D1562077

A PRIMER

HISTORY OF ROME

Wimbledon Publishing Company

Matt Melanson

A PRIMER HISTORY OF ROME
by Mandell Creighton

General editor: Professor John Traupman

Published by Wimbledon Publishing Company Ltd.
WPC Classics USA
4117 Hillsboro Pike, Suite 103-106
Nashville, TN 37215 USA

Fax: 801 749 2983

E-mail: sales@wpcpress.com

ISBN: 1898855 39 0

Produced in UK
Printed in Hungary

WPC Classics is an imprint of the Wimbledon Publishing Company
P.O. Box 9779, London SW19 7QA Fax: (+44) 20 8944 0825

CONTENTS

LIST OF MAPS AND TABLES

INTRODUCTION

How Roman History Explains Modern Europe

If we look at the nations of modern Europe, we at once notice that they differ very much from one another in language, laws, manners, and customs. Yet we see also, in spite of this difference, that they have a great likeness to one another, which distinguishes all of them from the nations of the other quarters of the world. Now the great thing which Roman history tells us is how these nations of Europe grew up, and how they came to be so different from one another, and yet how, though one nation differs from another, the people of Europe seem to be all almost the same, if we compare them with the people of Asia or Africa.

The great reason which makes the people of Europe have so much in common is that they all owe a great deal to the laws and customs and ideas of the Romans who conquered and governed them; and the reason why they differ from one another is that some owe more than others to the Romans; some have kept more of the ideas of the Romans; others have kept more of the ideas of the Germans, who broke up the government of the Romans and founded new nations in Europe. So you see that the history of Rome will explain to you how the nations of Europe grew up as they are at present.

How Roman History Teaches About Old Times

But besides seeing how the nations of Europe grew up under the influence of Rome, you will also see how the power of Rome was gained by conquering all the ancient nations. You will see how the people of Rome first of all overcame all the other people of Italy, and then went on to overcome all the nations that lived around the Mediterranean Sea. Also, besides conquering these nations, they governed them, gave them their own laws, and made them all like themselves in some degree or another. Now, these nations which lived around the Mediterranean Sea were the only peoples who lived in cities, made themselves laws, wrote books, and were what we in these times call *civilized.*

So you see Roman history teaches you something about all the great nations, both ancient and modern. Rome was a great link in the history of the world,—for all the ancient nations were conquered by Rome, and so came under Rome's power, while all the European nations of our own days were formed out of the overthrow of Rome, and learned a great deal from her.

Important Points in Roman History

These, then, are the important points for you to notice in Roman history:

➤ How did Rome become fit to be such a great conqueror?
➤ How did she make her conquests?
➤ How did she manage to keep her conquests?
➤ How did she govern the world when she was its mistress?
➤ Why did she fall?

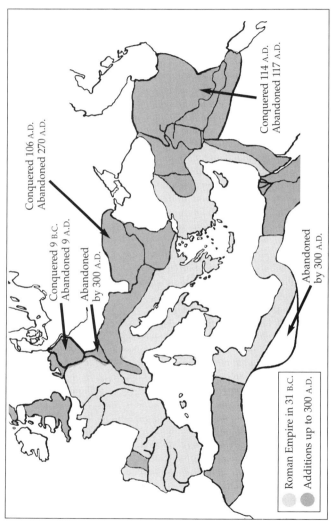

Conquered 114 A.D.
Abandoned 117 A.D.

Conquered 106 A.D.
Abandoned 270 A.D.

Conquered 9 B.C.
Abandoned 9 A.D.

Abandoned
by 300 A.D.

Abandoned
by 300 A.D.

Roman Empire in 31 B.C.

Additions up to 300 A.D.

The Roman Empire at its Greatest Extent

I

HOW ROME

BECAME A CITY

Italy in Early Times

Rome, as you know, is the capital of Italy; and Italy is the middle one of the three peninsulas which make the south of Europe and are washed by the Mediterranean Sea. Italy at present is bounded on the north by the Alps. But in the year 753 B.C., when Rome was founded, the great plain between the Alps and the Apennines, which we now call Lombardy, belonged to the Gauls and was called Gallia. Also, on the west coast between the Apennines and the Tiber river lived the Etruscans, who were the greatest people in the peninsula at that time. The land which they lived in is still called Tuscany after them.

South of the Gauls and Etruscans came the Italians, among whom the Latins were the principal race. The Latins lived in the plain south of the Tiber and were an agricultural people. They lived in villages, and each village managed its own affairs, but they all gathered together some-

Italy at the Time of Rome's Founding

times for common objects, and this gathering together was called a *league.*

Founding of Rome

It would seem that about the year 753 B.C. these Latins founded a colony on the Tiber to guard the river against the Etruscans, of whom they were afraid. This colony was called Rome, and as it was founded upon the great river of that part of Italy, it soon became of importance for trade, as well as for keeping off the Etruscans.

Roman Stories about Rome's Founding

Now this is all we can really know about the founding of Rome, but the Romans themselves tell this story about it. A wicked king called Amulius ruled in Alba Longa. He had robbed his elder brother Numitor of the kingdom and put his sons to death, but a daughter of his had twin sons, whose father was the god Mars. Amulius ordered them to be thrown into the Tiber river; but they floated down the stream till they stuck near the place where Rome was afterwards built. They were fed first by a shewolf, and afterwards were found and brought up by a shepherd. When they had grown up, they were made known to their grandfather, whom they restored to his throne after slaying the wicked Amulius. Then the youths, whose names were Romulus and Remus, determined to build a city on the Tiber. They quarreled whose city it should be, and Remus was killed in the quarrel. So Romulus built the city and called it Rome after his own name and was its first king, and made his city great in war. He was taken up to heaven by his father Mars and was worshipped by the Romans as a god.

After his disappearance the people elected as their king Numa Pompilius, who was a peaceful king, and gave them laws, and taught them religion. Then came a warlike king, Tullus Hostilius, who conquered and took Alba, not by a regular battle, but by a fight between three brothers on each side. The fourth king, Ancus Martius, still further increased Rome's power over the Latins.

Now these are no doubt mere stories, but this is quite certain, that all this time Rome was rising into importance, and though she was the youngest of the Latin settlements, she early became the head of the League (or gathering together) of Latin villages. So you see Rome was a conqueror from the very first.

The City of Rome

Rome was built on the banks of the Tiber river, about fifteen miles from its mouth. It consisted at first of only a few houses upon a little hill near the river, which had a wall built around it. But as the number of people who came there grew greater, other hills close by were added to the city, and the wall was carried around them also. Not more than 150 years after Rome's founding there were seven hills within the wall, which was nearly five miles around. So Rome was sometimes called "the city of the seven hills."

The People of Rome

The city grew in numbers because men came and lived within the wall to be safe from their enemies. Some of the men were merchants and went up and down the Tiber in their boats. But the greater part of them were farmers, who tilled the land which lay round about the city. So, by Rome you must always understand the city and the land around it. As fast as the city grew in number of citizens, the land it possessed grew also larger and larger. You see, then, that these citizens who lived together in Rome had to think how they could best keep off their enemies and save their lands from being plundered. The citizens living together for their common good form what is called a *State,* and the means taken to bring about that common good is called *the government* of the state.

How Rome Was Governed in Early Times.

At first Rome's government was very simple. The state consisted of a number of families, and each family was ruled by its head. For state matters the heads of the families, who were called *patres or fathers*, met together in the *Senate* or *meeting of the old men*. The king was the president of the Senate and was the father of the state, which was looked upon as a large family.

But as Rome became more important, many new people came there who had no place in the old families, and so had no share in the government. They were looked down upon by the *patres* and were called *the plebs,* or *crowd.* Thus Rome became an *aristocracy,* or *government of nobles,* and the common people *(plebeians),* having no share in the government, were badly treated by the patres *(patricians).* So Rome was at war within herself, and you must see how this war went on. It stopped Rome's conquests for a long while; she could not conquer others when she was torn in pieces herself.

How the Kingship Came to an End

So the next three kings after Ancus Martius had difficulties at home. First, Tarquinius Priscus, who also made war against the Latins, tried to make a few changes in the state but was prevented by the nobles. After him came Servius Tullius, who succeeded in helping the plebeians by making a new division of the people, according to their wealth. Then he ordered that every man should bear arms according to his possessions, and that men with the same arms should drill and serve together in *centuries,* that is, *bands* of *100 men.* As the army was of course very important in the state, many things about the government were settled in meetings of the *centuries.* Thus the rich men among the plebeians were now better off. But there was great discontent felt by the nobles, and the good king Servius was murdered by his son-in-law, Lucius Tarquinius, who succeeded him on the throne. The Romans have called him *Superbus,* or *the*

Proud, for he ruled them harshly, according to his will. He took advantage of their quarrels to make himself a *tyrant*, that is, one who governs by his own will, and not according to the laws of the state. He made himself the master instead of the father of the state. He was a great warrior and made Rome still more powerful in Latium. But at last the Romans could endure him no more, so they rose against him and drove him out with his whole family, and resolved that they would have no more kings.

This driving out of the kings took place in 509 B.C., after Rome had been governed by kings 244 years. But we cannot be sure about these kings or about the times when they lived, as there were no Roman writers till long after this time, and we cannot be certain about stories written three or four hundred years after the events they tell about.

Rome as a Republic

When the Romans determined to have no kings, they seem first to have given the position of king to one man, who held it for a year only and was called *Dictator*. Then, thinking this power was still too much for one man, they elected two yearly officers who were at first called *Praetors* (or *leaders*), and afterwards *Consuls* (or *deliberators*). They still, however, kept the office of dictator in reserve, and when the state was in great danger a dictator was specially appointed, who for six months might be sole magistrate and exercise the old kingly power over the state. The ordinary magistrates, however, were the consuls, who presided over the Senate and also led the army to battle. Of course, under yearly magistrates the Senate had more power than it had had under the kings; also, the assembly of the people, who were called together in their *centuries* according to their military array, became more important, and their consent was necessary in making laws.

Early Difficulties of the Republic

All this took some time to settle, and Rome was not as powerful at first as a Republic as she had been under her kings. She was attacked by the other Latin cities and by the Etruscans, and suffered great distress. Her lands were ravaged, and the Etruscans besieged, and seem even to have taken Rome. When at length they were driven back, the plebeians were in great misery. Most of them were farmers, whose farms had been entirely destroyed in the war. They themselves also had to serve in the army without receiving any pay and were called upon also to pay taxes when the state was in difficulties. We cannot, then, wonder that the plebeians ran into debt and borrowed money from the patricians, who seem to have wished to use their distress as a means of strengthening their own power in the state. The old law of debt was very strict and gave up the debtor entirely to his creditor, who might imprison him or sell him into slavery. The houses, therefore, of the patricians had prisons attached to them, which were full of plebeian debtors.

How the Plebeians Got their Own Magistrates

At last, in 494, only sixteen years after the expulsion of the kings, the plebeians thought that this state of things could not be borne any longer. So they marched out of Rome in a body and took up a position on a hill a few miles away from the city, declaring that they would found there a new plebeian city and leave the patricians to live in Rome by themselves. You may imagine the patricians did not like being left in this way, and so they sent to the plebeians a wise man, Menenius Agrippa, to persuade them to come back. He told them a fable: "Once upon a time the other members of the body conspired against the belly; they declared that they had to do all the work, while the belly lay quietly in the middle of the body and enjoyed without any labor everything they brought it. So they all went on strike and agreed to starve the belly into submission. But while they starved the belly, the whole body began to waste away, and all the members found that they were becoming weaker themselves. So you plebeians will find that in trying to starve out the patricians you will ruin yourselves." The plebeians thought there was much truth in this, and they agreed to go back on condition that they might have officers of their own to protect them.

These officers were called *Tribunes*, and their duty was to protect all plebeians from wrong. They could deliver any man from the patrician magistrates; their houses were to be places of refuge for anyone who was pursued; their doors were to stand open day and night. Moreover, anyone who laid hands upon them or tried to hurt them was to be outlawed. Their persons were to be sacred as those of heralds.

Thus you see a plebeian state, with the tribunes for its officers, had been founded by the side of the patrician state with its consuls. The quarrels of the two classes had gone so far that Rome was no longer one state, but two.

Struggles of the Patricians and Plebeians

You may imagine that this attempt to get over difficulties by making two states instead of one within the walls of Rome did not make Rome strong or likely to go on with her career as a conqueror. But you will remember that we said the first question to be answered about Rome was, How did she *become fit* to be such a great conqueror?

One great reason was that the first 200 years of the Roman Republic (500-300) were spent in a continual struggle between the patricians and plebeians. Both parties, to begin with, were very much attached to Rome and to its institutions. Each party regarded the other as fellow citizens, though they wished to oppose them on some particular point. The struggle was carried on with great moderation. There was very seldom bloodshed, and never civil war. They had enemies outside Rome whom they had to fight, and often they would lay aside their own quarrels when they were at the fiercest and go out together to battle.

What the Romans Learned from their Struggles

Now this was a good training for a great people. It taught them to be severe, yet just, at the same time. It gave every man a high sense of his duty to his fellow men, that is, to the state; it made him always do his best, for he always had something before him to do. The plebeians respected the patricians and knew that they could only overcome them by working hard for the common good and showing that they were worthy of the rights they asked for. The patricians held on to their own privileges as long as they could, but learned to know when they were beaten; when they could hold out no longer, they gave way and tried to make the best of it. In this way the Roman people learned obedience, self-control, and perseverance. But they learned not only to be wise in their own separate lives, but also to be wise in their general life together as fellow citizens and members of the same state. This "political wisdom," as it is called, helped them greatly afterwards. For though they held very fast to their old institutions, they learned that changes must sometimes be made, and they learned how to make them slowly and gradually, without disturbing more than could be helped the ordinary course of things. It was because they had learned how to give way when they had to give way, and how to make changes wisely and slowly, that the Romans became fit to govern the world when they had conquered it.

What the Patricians and Plebeians Strove About

Now we must speak of a few of the things which the patricians and plebeians fought about. Their strife lasted for nearly two hundred years, but you may divide this into two periods.

➤ 494-450 B.C. Fifty years, during which the plebeians were trying to escape from their misery.

➤ 450-300 B.C. A hundred and fifty years, in which the plebeians were trying to get as great a share in the government as the patricians.

Agrarian Law of Spurius Cassius

The first great attempt to make the plebeians less miserable was the *Agrarian Law* of Spurius Cassius, 486 B.C. Spurius Cassius was himself a patrician and had been consul, and when consul he had done good service to the state by making peace with the Latins, who were henceforth to be the equal allies of Rome. He saw the sad condition of the plebeians and the debts which they were obliged to run into, and which brought them to ruin and misery. He proposed, accordingly, that parcels of the *public land* should be divided among the poor plebeians. The public land was the land which had been won in war and belonged to the state.

Some of this land had been distributed to citizens when it was conquered, and some had been given to the temples to provide for the service of the gods whom the Romans worshipped. What was left belonged to the state; but the state meant as yet the patricians. So the patricians fed their cattle on this public land and used it as their own. What Spurius Cassius proposed was, that some of this land should be divided among the poor plebeians, and that the patricians who fed their cattle on the remainder should pay a rent to the state for doing so. It seems that this law was passed but was never carried into effect, for the patricians put difficulties in the way. They hated Spurius Cassius for his law and accused him of conspiring to make himself popular that so he might become a king, and on this charge they put him to death (485 B.C.). But this *Agrarian Law* was never forgotten, and you must remember what it was, for we shall hear of it again.

How the Tribunes Became Powerful

The misery after Cassius' death went on increasing, and the tribunes of the plebs became more important in consequence. The plebeians looked upon the tribunes as their own magistrates, and the tribunes used to call the plebeians together to discuss questions that arose. The plebeians came and voted according to their tribes when the tribunes called them together, though at first they could only pass resolutions but had no means of putting them into effect. The patricians did not like these meetings and tried to disturb them. But the plebeians only held to them the faster, so that they became more important. And now there were really two states in Rome. The consuls took counsel with the Senate and then made laws with the consent of the people in the Assembly of the Centuries. But the tribunes took counsel with the plebeians in the Assembly of the Tribes, and though they could not make laws, still they were very powerful. For, if the consuls made a law which the plebeians did not like, the tribunes could protect anyone who broke the law from being punished for breaking it; and so the law could not be carried into effect.

The Decemviri

You will see this state of things could not last long. In 461 the plebeians asked that the consuls and tribunes also should cease, and that ten new magistrates should be elected from the patricians and plebeians alike. These magistrates were to find out the laws, and post them in the *forum,* or *market place,* where the people gathered together, so that everyone should know them, and no man should be unjustly oppressed. Till this time the patricians had kept the laws to themselves, and so had been able to judge the plebeians as they chose. For ten years there were bitter struggles about this proposal, till, in 451, ten new magistrates, called *Decemviri,* or the *Ten Men,* were appointed. They published the laws, to the great joy of the plebeians. But one among the Decemviri, Appius Claudius, a patrician, was a proud and haughty man who would always have his own way. He wished to have for his servant the daughter of a plebeian called Virginius; so he got a man to declare that Virginia, as the girl was called, was not really the daughter of Virginius, but of a slave of his. The case was brought before Appius Claudius to try, and Appius of course decided that Virginia was a slave. Then her father, who was a soldier and had hurried to Rome from the camp, led his daughter to one side to say "Farewell" to her; but he seized a butcher's knife from the market place and plunged it into his daughter's heart, saying, "It is the only way to keep you free." Then the people in horror rose against Appius, drove out the Decemviri, and elected consuls and tribunes again.

Still the plebeians had now gotten the laws, and so grew more powerful, and after the Decemvirate (B.C. 450) they were not as wretched as they had been before.

How the Censors Were Made

From 450 to 300, when this struggle between the two orders came quite to an end, the plebeians were trying to get some of themselves made judges and rulers of the people, as the patricians were. In 450 the plebeians could not hold any office in the state, but by 300 they could hold any to which they were elected, and they had also secured some offices for themselves which might not be held by patricians. The chief office which the plebeians wished to be admitted to was the consulship. The patricians fought desperately to prevent this, and when they could hold out no longer, they weakened the power of the consuls by making new officers, who were to be patricians only. First, they made *Censors,* in 443, who were to hold office for five years; they were to take *a census* or *numbering of the people* and issue lists on which the rank of all the citizens was to depend. These censors could inquire into men's conduct and degrade them from their rank if they pleased, and so had great power. You will remember, too, that the numbering of the people is called a *Census* by us today and was always a custom of the Roman state; but with the Romans it meant an arrangement of the people in their ranks, as well as merely counting them. It shows how the Romans liked order in everything they did.

Power of the Assembly of the Tribes

About this time Rome was busy with wars, as you will see presently, and the plebeians, by being good soldiers abroad, went on gaining power at home. One way in which this power showed itself was in the importance gained by their meetings in the Assembly of the Tribes. The plebeians demanded that the resolutions they passed there should be the laws of the state as much as the laws made by the consuls and the Assembly of the Centuries. The patricians had been obliged to give way to this, but were always refusing to obey the laws made by this plebeian assembly. So the quarrel still went on.

The Laws of Licinius and Sextius

At last, in 376, two of the tribunes, called Gaius Licinius Stolo and Lucius Sextius, determined to win the consulship for the plebeians. They brought forward three laws and said they must be all carried at once. These three laws had something good for both the rich and poor plebeians; for many of the plebeians were now rich men, though they were still looked down upon by the old houses of the patricians. So all the plebeians, rich and poor alike, were now made to work together. The laws were these:

➤ That the poor should be helped to pay their debts.
➤ That when the poor were out of debt they should have parcels of the public land given them, and the rich should only be allowed to till or feed cattle on a certain part of it.
➤ That one of the consuls must always be a plebeian.

These great laws are called the Licinian-Sextian laws, from the name of their proposers. The patricians fought hard against them for ten years. But Licinius and Sextius were elected tribunes year after year and used their power as tribunes to the utmost. They prevented the election of any consuls or magistrates for five years, by saying that as tribunes they would protect everyone who disobeyed these magistrates; and so it was of no use to elect them. The patricians at last had to give way, and in 366 the first plebeian consul was elected.

End of the Struggle between Patricians and Plebeians

This year, 366, really marks the victory of the plebeians. They had, however, to fight on to get the patricians to keep these laws of Licinius and Sextius after they were passed. The law about the public land was soon forgotten, and the plebeians had to fight hard at first to keep their one consul. After this they forced the patricians to share with them all the other offices, and in the year 300 patricians and plebeians had equal rights in Rome as far as justice and government went. Really the plebeians had gotten more than the patricians, for they had the tribunes all to themselves, and the patricians had no magistrates of their own. Also one of the consuls *must* be a plebeian, and both *might* be, if the votes so fell out. So you see that the patricians, by trying too hard to keep everything to themselves, really lost in the long run.

This long struggle between the patricians and plebeians is very strange. You must remember that both parties lived in the same city and were always meeting one another in the streets. But there were very seldom mobs or riots or bloodshed. In their struggles they always used means which the laws allowed, and the plebeians obeyed the laws, even though they wished to alter them. Both sides fought hard, yet kept their temper. They were not in a hurry, for they knew the strongest side would win at last.

How Rome Became
Mistress of Italy

The Peoples of Italy

During the time of this struggle between the patricians and plebeians, Rome could not become a very great nation. Still she was making herself feared in Italy, and it was partly because the plebeians fought so well against Rome's enemies that the patricians gave way to them at last.

To understand Rome's wars you must know clearly who the people around her were. You remember that south of the Alps were the Gauls; then along the west coast, north of Rome, were the Etruscans; while on the east coast, south of Rome, were a number of prosperous cities which were colonies founded by settlers from Greece. There were great and rich Greek cities too along the coast of Sicily. The rest of Italy was inhabited by purely Italian tribes, of which the Latins around Rome were one. But these Italian tribes were very different in habits and temper from one another, and

25

The Races of Italy

there were some warlike tribes living in the valleys of the Apennines, of whom the Latins were very much afraid.

Rome's Early Wars

Now, in 494 Spurius Cassius the consul made an alliance between Rome and the Latins, which another tribe, the Hernicans, joined soon after. These three allies defended themselves against their enemies. But Rome had very little power at first, and up to the year 405 was engaged in fighting against two tribes, called the Aequians and Volscians, who lived close by. The map will show you how near these tribes were to Rome, and how small

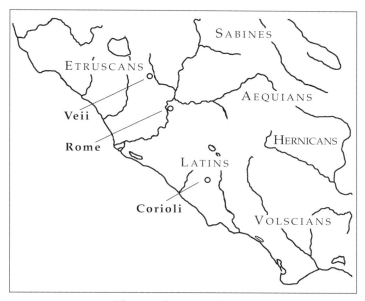

The Peoples around Rome

Rome's territory was at first. We know very little about these wars, but two stories are told about them which are worth knowing.

Story of Gaius Marcius Coriolanus

The story of Gaius Marcius Coriolanus shows you how the quarrels at home made Rome weak and it shows you, too, how the Romans were taught to obey their parents. Gaius Marcius was a patrician and a great soldier. He was once with the Roman army besieging the Volscian town, Corioli. The Volscians came out to fight but were driven back, and Gaius Marcius pursued them into their town. But he was the only Roman who did so, and so was shut in alone among the enemy. He was, however, so brave that he drove the Volscians by himself away from the gates and then opened the gates to the Roman army. So Corioli was taken, and the name of *Coriolanus,* or the *man of Corioli,* was given to Gaius Marcius for his valor.

After this there was a great famine at Rome, and when grain came from Sicily the Senate wished to sell it to the poor plebeians. But Gaius Marcius said, "Let them have no grain till they obey the patricians." Now the plebeians heard this and were very angry, and the tribunes brought Gaius Marcius to trial before them. Gaius knew he would be found guilty, and so he fled to the king of the Volscians and offered to serve him. Then the king of the Volscians gave him a large army, and he marched against Rome. The Romans were afraid and sent to ask for peace. They sent first the chief senators who had been the friends of Gaius Marcius, but he refused to listen to them. They then sent the priests with the images of the gods, but Gaius would not hear them either. Then the Romans were in great distress and had no hope of escape, till someone said, "Perhaps he will listen to his mother and his wife." Then his mother and his wife and children, with many of the chief ladies in Rome, went out dressed in mourning garments. And when Gaius saw his mother, he ran to meet her, but she said, "Do not kiss me till I know whether you are an enemy or a son." Then his mother and wife and children fell on their knees and begged him to spare Rome. And he wept and said, "Mother, this is a happy victory for you and Rome, but it is ruin and shame to your son." So he led his army back and Rome was saved. And soon after this he died among the Volscians.

Story of Lucius Quinctius Cincinnatus

Another story which the Romans tell of a war against the Aequians shows how simple their customs were, and how all the citizens served the state. The consul Minucius was warring against the Aequians, but they had shut him up in a steep narrow valley and guarded the mouth of it so that he could not get out. News was brought to Rome, and the Senate said, "There is only one man who can help us; let us make Lucius Quinctius dictator." So they sent messengers to Lucius Quinctius, whose surname was *Cincinnatus*, or *the curly-haired*. He was at his farm on which he lived, and was ploughing without his cloak when the messengers of the Senate found him. So he called to his wife to bring him his cloak that he might show respect to the messengers. They then hailed him as dictator and brought him to Rome. And he ordered all who could bear arms to get ready to march and to take with them provisions and twelve long stakes of wood. So he marched out with his army and came upon the Aequians by night. His soldiers raised a shout, which cheered the consul and his men, who knew that help had come, and so fell upon the Aequians. But Lucius bade his men dig a ditch around the Aequians and make a hedge around them with their wooden stakes. This they did all night, and when it was morning the Aequians found themselves shut in in their turn. Then they surrendered to the dictator; and so he rescued the consul and his army, and came back to Rome in triumph. But he laid down his office of dictator at once and went back to his farm.

Men like Lucius Quinctius, who left the plough and became generals when the state wanted them, and then went back contented to the plough again, were the men who won Rome's battles for her and made her great.

Wars with the Etruscans

These wars with the Aequians and Volscians were troublesome to Rome, but were not really great wars. Rome also had to watch her old enemies the Etruscans, for Rome, you remember, had been founded that she might keep the Etruscans away from the Latins. These Etruscans were a great people, who lived in cities and built large buildings, and made many beautiful things. They were great traders also, and had ships, and in early times they and the Carthaginians had been masters of the Mediterranean Sea. But the Greeks in Sicily and Italy, who wanted to trade in these seas as well, had fought both against the Etruscans and Carthaginians; and in a great battle in 474 the Etruscans had been terribly beaten at sea by the Greeks. But the Etruscans were also attacked on land by the Gauls in the north, and so their power began to grow less. When the Romans saw this, they attacked them on the south, and in 405 began the siege of the nearest Etruscan city, the city of Veii. For ten years the siege lasted, but at last a great general of the Romans named Marcus Furius Camillus took it. Then he went on and took many other Etruscan towns, till Rome's territory reached to the Ciminian hills. But Camillus was an honorable man, and when he was besieging Falerii there came one day into his camp a schoolmaster out of the town, bringing with him all his boys, who were the sons of the chief citizens of the town. These boys he brought to Camillus, that when he had them in his power, he might force their fathers to surrender to him. But Camillus was very angry, had the schoolmaster's hands tied behind his back, and ordered all the boys to flog him back again into the town and tell his baseness. Then the people of Falerii thought so highly of Camillus that they surrendered to him of their own accord.

The Romans Defeated by the Gauls

But the Romans soon suffered a great defeat, the great-est they ever met with. For the Gauls had also been con-quering the Etruscans from the north, while the Romans were attacking them from the south. But the Romans tried to help the Etruscans against them; then the Gauls marched against the Romans, defeated them on the River Allia (390), and advanced against Rome itself.

Rome Taken by the Gauls

The Romans had lost so many men in the battle that they had no hope of defending the city. So the people all fled, except a few of the bravest soldiers, who shut themselves up in the *Capitol,* which was the *fortress* or *castle* of Rome, determined that it should not be taken. There stayed also some of the oldest patricians, who would not leave in their old age the city they loved so well. They all dressed them-selves in their best robes and sat on their seats in the senate building. When the Gauls rushed in and found no one in the city except these old men who sat in silence, they were astonished. At last one of the Gauls began to stroke the long white beard of Marcus Papirius, who was one of the priests. He in anger struck the Gaul with his ivory scepter which he held in his hand. Then the Gauls rushed upon them and killed them all and set fire to the city. Next the Gauls tried to take the Capitol, but they could not find any way up to it because the rock was steep. At last they found a path, and one night a band of Gauls climbed up so secretly that no one of the Romans heard them. But there were in the Capitol some geese, which were sacred to the goddess Juno; and as the Gauls reached the top, these geese began to cackle and awoke a brave Roman, Marcus Manlius, who was just in time to find the foremost Gaul clambering over the edge of the rock. He pushed him back with his shield, and the Gaul fell; as he fell he knocked over many of those who were following him, and the Romans had time to wake up and drive the rest back. So the Capitol was saved; and after a while the Gauls went back to their own country, carrying their plunder with them.

Effects of This Burning of Rome

Now this taking and burning of Rome by the Gauls is no doubt the reason why we know so little with certainty of the early history of Rome. For in those days the priests kept notes of all that happened every year, and stored them in their temples. So, when the temples were burnt by the Gauls, all these notes and chronicles must have been burnt with them, and we cannot feel very certain about anything that happened before this time. But after this, things begin to get more certain, and we know more of what the Romans were really doing.

Marcus Manlius and the Plebeians

Then the Romans came back and found their city in ruins, and at first they talked of leaving Rome and going to live in Veii. But Camillus persuaded them to stay and build their city again. This was a heavy burden on the poor plebeians, and they suffered great misery and were in great debt. One day a brave soldier was being dragged off to prison for debt, when Marcus Manlius, who had saved the Capitol, dismayed at this, paid the debt for him and saved him. Manlius said also that so long as he had any money he would not see a citizen made a slave for debt. The plebeians loved him for this; but the patricians were afraid of him.

Rome and the Samnites

They accused him of trying to make himself a king, and put him to death (383). So the plebeians learned they must look to laws to protect them and not to men.

Effects of the Coming of the Gauls

This invasion of the Gauls was not really a great disaster to the Romans. They suffered, it is true, but not as much as their old enemies the Aequians, who from this time forward troubled the Romans no more. Also the Romans learned to improve their armies and to be more careful in battle. The Gauls came back from their country along the Po year after year and plundered wherever they went; but the Romans never again went out to fight them rashly. They drove them little by little, till the Gauls were afraid to come back again. After the year 350 we hear no more of their invasions, but Rome had grown in power by her wars with them and was looked up to by all the tribes round about as their protector.

Beginning of the Samnite Wars

The Gauls had crushed others besides the Aequians, especially the Greek cities south of Rome in the district called Campania. These cities were so weak and also so wealthy that, when the Gauls were gone, they were attacked by a hardy Italian tribe, called the Samnites, who lived among the Apennine mountains, which ran down the center of Italy. The Samnites so distressed one of these cities, Capua, that she called on the Romans to help her in the year 343. This was the beginning of the Samnite wars, which lasted for more than 50 years, that is, to the year 290.

This time of the Samite wars was a most important time for Rome; it settled whether Rome was to govern Italy or not. The Samnites were the stoutest and bravest enemies Rome had yet met with; they were as stubborn, and almost as strong as the Romans themselves. The first Samnite war was soon over and had not much result; both sides were willing to make peace, especially Rome, for she was just then afraid of her allies, the Latins.

The Latin War

The Latins, now that the Gauls were gone, did not wish to be subject to the Romans any more. In 340 they sent to the Romans and asked to be made equal with them. They were willing that Rome should still be the capital of the alliance, but its Senate must be doubled, and there must be two Latin as well as two Roman Consuls every year. The Romans would not agree to this, and so the great Latin war arose, which was to settle which of these two powers, the Romans or the Latins, should rule the other. It lasted three years (340-338) and was very severe. The greatest battle of the war was fought at the foot of Mount Vesuvius, and victory was for a long time doubtful. But the Roman consul, Publius Decius Mus, had heard that that side should conquer whose general gave himself up to death. So he covered his head with his cloak, and rushing among the enemy, was killed. Then the victory went slowly in favor of the Romans.

The Doom of Manlius

You may judge how stern the Romans were by a story told of the other consul, Titus Manlius. He had given orders that no one should fight a single combat with any of the foe. One day, however, his own son, being challenged by an enemy, fought with him and killed him and brought back his spoils. His father ordered him to be beheaded for disobedience and stood by to see it done. And though all men were struck with horror, yet they said that the doom of Manlius was just.

How Rome Governed the Latins

The Latins, then, were conquered, and Rome took all their towns, gave them different privileges, and taught them all to look up to Rome herself, and to care more for her than they had done for one another. You see, Rome could not look upon the Latins as strangers, for they had long been her allies. Romans and Latins had fought side by side, used the same arms, and been almost brothers. So when Rome conquered, she did not treat the Latins harshly, but she took care that they should not rise against her again. So she would not allow the Latin cities to trade with one another, but made them all trade with Rome so that Rome became their capital. Also she gave them all hopes of being made citizens of Rome if they remained faithful. So the Latins began to forget that they had been conquered and were proud of being ruled by Rome. Rome learned in this way how to bind to herself the people she conquered, so that they seldom tried to rebel. You must remember that later on she always did the same things after a war: she separated the towns she had won from one another and made them all hope that she would reward them if they were only true to her.

Second Samnite War

It was well for Rome that she had made the Latins contented, for in 327 began the second Samnite war, which lasted till 305, for twenty-two years. It was a war in which both sides fought hard, for they knew that the people which won would be the chief state in Italy. The Samnites had a very brave general, called Gaius Pontius, who once very nearly destroyed the Roman army. He made his army pretend to run away, and the Romans followed him by the shortest way, till they were shut up in a valley, with the Samnites all around them, and could not get out. They had to surrender to Pontius, and he made peace with them and let them go free. But the Romans at home would not hear of the peace; they said that no peace was rightly made except by the Senate, and they sent back as prisoners to Pontius the consuls who had made the peace. Pontius said he might have killed all the army if he had chosen, and then he could have forced them to make peace; now, if they would not have

Rome and South Italy

peace, let them put their army back again in the pass of Caudium. But the Romans refused, saying they had sent him the consuls who had done the wrong, and that was all they were bound to do. Pontius sent the consuls back, and the war went on. The Romans did not act fairly in this, but they were always a people who thought they had done their duty if they kept the letter of the law.

As the war went on, the Etruscans became frightened of Rome's power and helped the Samnites, but they too were beaten. At last, in 304, the Samnites were obliged to lay down their arms.

Third Samnite War

But peace did not last long, for in 300 began the third Samnite war. All the peoples of Italy who up to this time had been fighting against one another were now drawn together by a common dread of Rome, and so this war was a desperate struggle of Samnites, Etruscans, and Gauls to shake off the power of Rome. A great battle was fought in 295 at Sentinum, in which the Romans beat them all. Two years afterwards the brave leader of the Samnites, Gaius Pontius, was taken prisoner by the Romans, who had no pity for him, but put him to death. The Romans always showed themselves without mercy for those who rose against them, and this was another reason why the towns they conquered did not often rise again.

Wars with the Greek Cities

Now, the last Samnite war had settled that Rome was to be mistress of all southern Italy. She had subdued the Samnites and Etruscans, and had driven back the Gauls, and there were only some Greek cities in the south to stand against her. These cities had once been very powerful, and were still very rich, in fact so rich that they did not care about fighting for themselves. One of the most important of these cities was Tarentum, on the great gulf of Tarentum in the south of Italy. The Romans had been helping some of the other cities near Tarentum against their enemies, and the people of Tarentum were very jealous of Rome's power. One day the people were all sitting in the theater, which was in the open air and had its seats looking towards the sea. They were listening to one of those plays of which the Greeks were so fond, when suddenly they saw ten Roman ships sail close to the harbor of Tarentum. In a rage they rushed to their ships, attacked the Romans, and destroyed half of them. So the war began in the year 282.

War with Pyrrhus

But the Tarentines were afraid of fighting for themselves, and there was no people in Italy strong enough to fight against Rome. So they turned to Greece, and asked help from Pyrrhus, King of Epirus, which was on the west coast of Greece and the nearest part to Italy. Pyrrhus was very glad to come and help them; for he was young, and wished to be a great conqueror; he was a good general, and brought a large army of good soldiers. It was a serious thing for the Romans to begin to fight with nations which lived outside of Italy, but they had to do it in their own defense.

In 280 Pyrrhus landed in Italy with a large army. The Romans who went against him were defeated at Heraclea, on the little river Siris. Their cavalry was not nearly as good as that of the Greeks, and their horses were frightened at the sight of some elephants which the Greeks had brought with them. But though Pyrrhus won the battle, he lost so many men that he said, "A few more such victories, and I am ruined." So he sent to Rome to try to make peace on good terms for himself and Tarentum. He sent a very clever man, called Cineas, who almost persuaded the Senate; but a Roman noble, who had been consul and censor but was now old and blind, had himself carried to the senate building, and with his dying breath begged them never to make peace as long as Pyrrhus stayed in Italy. Then the Senate sent Cineas away with this answer; and when he came to Pyrrhus he said, "It is useless to fight with Rome, for its Senate is an assembly of kings." Next year Pyrrhus defeated the Romans again, but they would not give way. So

Pyrrhus went over to Sicily and fought there for two years. Then when he came back his army was much weaker. The Romans meanwhile had been learning to improve their cavalry and to fight against elephants; and so they could meet Pyrrhus more equally. So in 275 a battle was fought at Beneventum, in which Pyrrhus was beaten by the Romans. He had to go back again to Epirus, having lost almost all his troops. His hopes of conquest were at an end, and three years afterwards he was killed in Greece by a stone thrown on his head by a woman while he was besieging Argos.

Rome's Government of Italy

After Pyrrhus had been driven away, Rome had no difficulty in taking all south Italy. And now Rome ruled all south of a line drawn between the little river Macra on the west coast, and the Rubicon on the east coast. North of this lay Gaul. Rome was herself a city, and she ruled over the cities which she had taken, for the country in Italy was all divided into districts belonging to the cities. The state of things, then, in Italy was this: the citizens of Rome governed all the rest, and everyone wished to become a citizen of Rome. Next to the Romans came the Latins, who had some of the rights of Roman citizenship and hoped to get the other rights in time. Then below the Latins came the Italians, who governed their own cities in which they lived but had to obey Rome and serve in Rome's armies when they were wanted.

There were two ways by which Rome kept Italy under her power. You must notice them, as they are the ways which she always used afterwards with her conquests. The ways were these

➤ She founded colonies.
➤ She made roads.

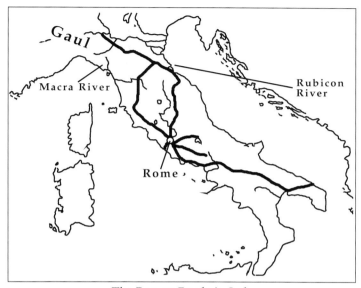

The Roman Roads in Italy

Rome's Colonies

Colonies, as you know, are *settlements made in foreign countries.* The Romans took some of the land of the people they conquered in Italy, and sent some Roman citizens to live on it, and form themselves into a state. Thus a number of little Romes were scattered about Italy; and Rome could always trust her colonists, as a Roman never forgot Rome. These colonies were almost garrisons to keep the Italians in order; but they were much better than garrisons of soldiers, for they were garrisons of peaceful men, who worked hard at their farms and taught others to do so as well. Thus the Italians learned to know the Romans, and tried to be like them, and were content to be governed by Rome.

Roman Roads

The Romans were great builders of roads. They made them so well and so strong that some Roman roads still remain in use at the present day. These roads went from Rome to different parts of Italy, and so Rome could send soldiers where they were wanted and could get news quickly. This was very useful as a way of keeping order. You will see from the map how they were spread over Italy and served as so many chains by which Rome fastened other cities to herself.

Character of the Old Romans

In this way, then, Rome governed Italy. And these days of her wars with the Samnites and with Pyrrhus were her most flourishing days. For the Romans still had to work hard and had not yet grown rich; and so they were honest and brave and noble. Many stories are told showing how simply the old Romans lived. Their great generals and statesmen were no grander than other people, and when presents were sent them, they used to refuse to take them. Thus, the Samnites sent a present of gold to a great Roman general, Manius Curius. The messengers found him at his farm, cooking his own dinner, which was a turnip roasted in the ashes of his fire, and he had only a wooden dish to eat it on. When the Samnites brought out their gold, Curius refused to take it, saying, "It is more glorious not to have gold, but to have power over those who have it."

But the time was soon to come when the Romans were to grow rich from foreign wars, and their simple life would last no longer.

Rome's Wars

with Carthage

Only eleven years after Pyrrhus had gone, the Romans were engaged in another war with foreigners, with the Carthaginians.

Origin of Carthage

Carthage, as you will see on the map, was a town on the north coast of Africa, at the point where the African coast is nearest to Sicily. Carthage itself was a colony of the Phoenicians, who lived on the coast of Syria just above Palestine, and whose great towns were Tyre and Sidon. These Phoenicians were the same people as the Canaanites who had been driven out of Palestine by the Israelites. They spoke Hebrew and so belonged to the same great Semitic race to which the Jews also belonged. In ancient times they had been great traders; their ships are said to have sailed as far as Gaul, and brought tin overland from Britain. Carthage is said to have been founded as a colony

Rome and Carthage

of Tyre about 100 years before the foundation of Rome, but it grew into power sooner than Rome did because it was engaged in trade. Carthage was like Rome in not being ruled by a king, but it was ruled by its nobles, who were very rich from the money they gained in trade. All the western half of the north coast of Africa had been conquered by Carthage, but the conquered people were not treated by them as well as the Italians were by Rome. You will see how important this was in the great war that was now coming on.

Carthaginians in Sicily

It was in Sicily that the Romans and Carthaginians first met one another. It was very natural that they should do so, as the island of Sicily lies between Italy and Carthage. The Sicels, who gave their name to Sicily, were an Italian people, very like the Latins at first. But the Greeks planted colonies in Sicily as early as 735, and the Sicels learned to be like the Greeks. These Greeks were great traders as well as the Carthaginians, and so the two were always fighting, especially as the Carthaginians settled on the west coast of Sicily and tried to drive out the Greeks. Thus, while Rome was carrying on her early wars in Italy, there was constant fighting in Sicily between the Carthaginians and the Greeks under the tyrants or kings of Syracuse.

First Punic War

The cause of these *Phoenician,* or *Punic* wars, as the wars with Carthage are called, was this. Some Italian pirates had settled in Messana, the nearest city in Sicily to Italy. Both the Greeks and Carthaginians wished to drive them out, and so the pirates called to Rome for help, and Rome, not wishing the Carthaginians to take Messana, sent help; and so a war began which was to last for twenty-two years (264-241).

The Romans had no ships, while the Carthaginians, being great traders, had a large fleet. But the Romans had a better army on land, as every Roman was a soldier, and the Italians who were in Rome's army fought willingly for Rome. The Carthaginians sent generals only of their own with an army hired from the peoples under their rule, who cared for nothing but their pay.

Growth of Rome's Navy

At first, when the war was carried on in Sicily, the Romans drove back the Carthaginians, and compelled the Greek king of Syracuse to make peace, and ally himself with them instead of with Carthage. But the Carthaginian ships did so much harm to the Italian coast that the Romans saw they could do nothing till they also had a fleet. It happened that a Carthaginian ship was wrecked on the shore of Italy. So the Romans took it as a model and began to build ships like it. And at the same time that they were building the ships, they began to train rowers. Ships in those days were rowed by men arranged in rows one above the other; and in large warships there were five such rows,—so that it required some practice before the ships could be used. In 260 the new fleet put to sea. The Romans knew they could conquer if they could only have a chance of close fighting; and so they had long wooden bridges fastened to their masts, with a spike at the end. When their ships came near enough to the Carthaginian ships, the bridge was let fall, and the spike fixed it in the deck of the ship on which it fell. Then the Roman soldiers ran on board the Carthaginian ship and easily took it. By this means the Romans, though they were not good seamen, won two great battles at sea in the next four years.

Regulus in Africa (256)

Made bold by this, the Roman consul, Marcius Regulus, sailed to Africa and plundered all the country. The Carthaginians were very frightened and offered to make peace, but Regulus would have nothing but entire submission. Then the Carthaginians gathered an army, fell upon the Romans and defeated them, and took Regulus prisoner. Still the war went on as before in Sicily, and in 250 the Romans won a battle and took prisoners some Carthaginian nobles. The Carthaginians, wishing to get them back, sent Regulus to Rome and made him promise that, if he did not make an exchange of prisoners, he would come back to Carthage. Regulus thought that the Romans would lose by the exchange, and he boldly said so, and advised the Senate not to make it. So they refused, and Regulus nobly kept his word, and left his wife and children and friends in Rome, and went back to die in prison at Carthage.

End of the First Punic War

The war dragged on till 241, when the Romans won a great victory at sea. The Carthaginians were tired and wished for peace. There had arisen also among them a great general, Hamilcar, surnamed *Barca,* or *Lightning*, who saw that Carthage must have some time of quiet in which she might train soldiers who could fight the Romans on land. So the Carthaginians made peace, and agreed to pay Rome a large sum of money and to leave her Sicily. Peace was therefore made, but neither side meant that it should last long; both wanted time to get ready for a new war.

Rome's First Province

Rome had now gained her first possession outside Italy, that is, Sicily. A few years afterwards she forced the Carthaginians to give up to her the islands of Sardinia and Corsica. She did not treat the people of Sicily in the same way as she had treated the people of Italy. But she made Sicily what was called a *province,* which meant, a country governed by a Roman magistrate. The people of Sicily, then

had no share in the government of Rome, nor had they any
hope of ever having any. They were not the *allies* of Rome,
but her *subjects.* They were governed by magistrates sent
every year from Rome, and they had to pay *tribute* to Rome,
that is a sort of rent for their land.

This way of governing Sicily was afterwards used by
Rome for all the peoples she conquered; and so you must
remember it carefully. Rome governed the Latins in one
way, the Italians in another, and the people of the provinces
in a third.

Carthaginians in Spain

We saw that the first war with Carthage came to an end
because both sides were tired and because Hamilcar wanted to get an army ready with which he might fight the
Romans. He got the Carthaginians to send him to Spain,
and there he taught his soldiers how to fight hard; for Spain
was full of tribes of poor and brave men, who fought very
hard before they were conquered. Before Hamilcar left
Carthage he offered a great sacrifice to the gods; and as he
was offering, he called his young son Hannibal, who was
only nine years old, and asked him if he would like to go to
the war. Hannibal said "Yes." "Then," said his father,
"swear on this altar that you will never be the friend of the
Roman people." And the boy swore it and went with his
father, and you will see how he never forgot his promise.

Hamilcar fought in Spain till he died, and conquered for
Carthage all of Spain up to the river Tagus. When he died
his son-in-law Hasdrubal went on with his conquests, till
he was killed in 221, and Hannibal became general of the
army at the age of twenty-six.

The Romans meanwhile had not been idle; they had had
a great war with the Gauls in the north and had driven

them back to the great river of north Italy, the Padus, or Po. They had also made a treaty with Carthage that she should not conquer in Spain north of the river Iberus, which is now called Ebro.

How the Second Punic War Began

In the year 219 Hannibal thought he was fit to fight the Romans, and he began his great war with them, which lasted for seventeen years (219-202). The way in which he began it was this. There was a city on the east coast of Spain called Saguntum, which was a colony of the Greeks. Saguntum was afraid of the power of Carthage and had made a treaty with Rome that she should be Rome's ally. But Hannibal quarreled with Saguntum and besieged it, and the people fought hard against him. At last, after a siege of eight months, the chief men of the city, seeing they could hold out no longer, lit a great fire and threw into it all their treasures, and last of all threw themselves in as well. So Saguntum was taken. Then the Romans sent to Carthage to complain, and one of their ambassadors came before the Carthaginian senate holding his cloak together as if he were carrying something in it and he said, "I bring you peace or war; take whichever you like." The Carthaginians said, "Give us whichever you will." Then he shook his cloak open and said, "I give you war." And the Carthaginians shouted and said, "So let it be."

Hannibal's Plans

Now, Hannibal did not mean to fight this war by sea, but he meant to march his army at once into Italy and attack the Romans in their own country. He thought that the Gauls, who had so recently been conquered by Rome,

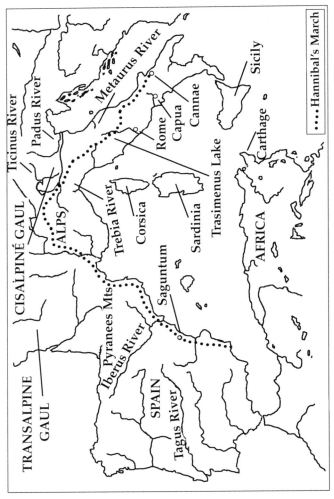

Hannibal's March to Italy

would dislike her very much and would be ready to rise up against her. He thought also that if he beat the Romans in one or two battles, all the ltalians would come over to his side, and so Rome would have to give in.

Hannibal's Difficulties

It was hard, however, to get into Italy at all, for he had first to go across the Pyrenees mountains to get out of Spain; then he had to cross the great river Rhodanus (Rhone), which was not easy to do, as the river is very swift, and the Gallic tribes on this side of the Alps, who did not want Hannibal to march through their country, tried to prevent him. Then he had to fight his way through these Gauls till he came to the Alps; and then he had to go with his army through the cold and snow and ice, and all the dangers which there are in crossing those high mountains. All this had to be done before he could reach the country of the Cisalpine Gauls, which we now call Lombardy, and the Romans also were sure to try to prevent him.

It is because he had all these difficulties to get over that Hannibal's march to Italy is so very famous. The Romans might have attacked him while he was among the Gauls, who dwelled west of the Alps, and so he would never have gotten into Italy at all. But he was too quick for them and moved so much faster than the Romans thought he would that they always came too late. Thus, the Roman army came to the Rhodanus just three days after Hannibal had crossed it, and so they had to go away and wait for him in Cisalpine Gaul, or Lombardy.

Hannibal's March to Italy

Hannibal crossed the Rhodanus very quickly; in two days he got together all the boats he wanted to take his soldiers across. The Gauls were on the opposite shore to prevent him from landing. So he sent some soldiers by night to go farther up the river and cross where the Gauls did not see them. Then he moored all his large boats so as to break the force of the stream and put his men in smaller boats, with the horses swimming by the side. So Hannibal waited till he saw some smoke rising behind the Gauls, for this was the sign that his soldiers who had been sent ahead had gotten across. Then he told all his men to row hard in their boats. As they got to the shore the Gauls rushed on them, but they heard a shout behind, and saw their tents on fire and the soldiers of Hannibal coming against them where they did not expect it. They were afraid and ran away, and so the soldiers landed easily. It was a much harder thing for Hannibal to march up the Alps, for the people of the mountains rolled down great stones upon his troops and attacked them from behind when they were not expecting. But even this was not as bad as the cold and the dangers of the snow and ice. These were most felt on the way down into Cisalpine Gaul; the paths, being only made of ice, broke away, and men slipped down the steep sides of the mountain and were killed. You can imagine how hard a march this was, when you know that Hannibal had 59,000 men when he crossed the Rhodanus, and when he got to the bottom of the Alps he had only 26,000 men.

Hannibal Defeats the Romans

You may suppose the Romans wanted to stop him as soon as possible, for the Cisalpine Gauls, who lived along the valleys of the Padus or Po, as Hannibal had hoped, began to join his army. The first battle was fought (218) on the river Ticinus, which runs into the Padus from the north. The Romans were driven back, and Hannibal passed the Padus. Meanwhile another Roman army had come up, and its general, the consul Tiberius Sempronius Longus, wanted to fight at once. The little river of the Trebbia lay between the two armies, and on a cold morning the Roman general marched his soldiers through the water against Hannibal. The Romans were entirely beaten and driven out of Gaul.

All of northern Italy had thus passed under Hannibal's power, and its people became his friends; so next year, 217, Hannibal went into Etruria and marched south towards Rome itself, plundering as he went. The Roman consul Gaius Flaminius Nepos went against him, and a battle was fought on the shores of the Lake Trasimenus. It was a misty day, and the Romans, who were marching after Hannibal, were surrounded by him and taken by surprise; they were thoroughly beaten, and the consul was killed in battle. Then the Romans were in great distress and elected a dictator, Quintus Fabius Maximus. He saw that it was no use to fight battles with Hannibal, so he followed him about, watched him, and did little things against him when he could; and so he was called *Cunctator,* or *the Delayer.*

Battle of Cannae

But, although this plan of waiting was very useful, the Romans did not like it, for Hannibal was left to plunder as he thought fit, and there was always danger that the other Italians would join him against Rome. So next year, 216, the Romans made a great attempt to get rid of him. They sent both the consuls with an army twice as large as Hannibal's, but again they were defeated at Cannae. They lost 70,000 men while Hannibal only lost 6,000; all their best soldiers were killed, and it seemed as though they had no hope left.

Rome's Strength in the War

But nations are not conquered only by the loss of battles. Hannibal hoped, after the battle of Cannae, that the Italians would all come over to his side and leave Rome. Some did so, but all the Latin cities and all the Roman colonies remained loyal to Rome. So long as this was the case, Rome was not yet conquered. Hannibal could win battles very quickly, but it would take him a long time to besiege all the cities that still were loyal to Rome, and for that he must have a larger army. But he could not get more soldiers—the Romans had sent an army into Spain, and Hannibal's brother, Hasdrubal, was busy fighting the Romans there and could not send any troops to Italy. The Carthaginians also would not send any, for they were becoming afraid of Hannibal, and they did not know anything about Italy. So they ignored his letters asking for more men, by saying that if he had won such great battles that he ought not to want any more troops.

At Cannae, then, Hannibal had struck his greatest blow; he could do no more. The Romans had learned to wait and be careful; and so they fought no more great battles, but every year they grew stronger while Hannibal grew weaker. The chief town that had gone over to Hannibal's side was Capua, but in 211 the Romans took it again, and Hannibal was not strong enough to prevent them. The chief men of Capua were so afraid of falling into the hands of the Romans that they all poisoned themselves. After this all the Italian cities that had joined Hannibal began to leave him again.

Defeat of Hasdrubal

At last, in 207, Hasdrubal managed to leave Spain and march across the Alps, bringing help to his brother. He marched along the east coast of Italy to join Hannibal in the south. But his messengers who were to tell his brother that he was coming fell into the hands of the Romans; and the consul, Gaius Claudius Nero, who was watching Hannibal in the south, marched up secretly to join the other consul in the north. Then Hasdrubal was defeated and killed on the banks of the river Metaurus, and Nero marched back again and threw Hasdrubal's head into Hannibal's camp. It was the first news he had had that his brother was in Italy, and it told him that now he could never hope to conquer Rome.

Rise of Scipio

Still Hannibal did not leave Italy, nor did the Romans try to drive him out, but they carried on the war elsewhere, and at last found a general who was a match for Hannibal. In 209 Publius Cornelius Scipio, whose father and grandfather had been Roman generals, was sent to Spain; there he won over the people by his kindness from the side of Carthage to that of Rome. After Hasdrubal's death the Romans grew still stronger in Spain, and in 206 the Carthaginians were entirely driven out by Scipio.

Battle of Zama

When Scipio came back to Rome he had made a plan for invading Africa, and so he got himself made consul and landed in Africa in 204. He destroyed the Carthaginian army by setting fire to their tents by night and killing them as they tried to run away. After this loss the Carthaginians were forced to recall Hannibal from Italy. In 202 a great battle was fought between him and Scipio at Zama. The battle was long and bloody, but Scipio had better cavalry, and they drove away Hannibal's cavalry and then fell upon his infantry in the rear. This was nearly all cut to pieces, and Hannibal's army was destroyed.

End of Hannibal

After this, of course, Carthage had to make peace; she had to pay great sums of money to Rome and promised never again to make war without asking permission from Rome. Hannibal still tried to help his country, but the Romans were afraid of him; so he was forced to flee from Carthage and then went from one king to another till he died. All the kings were afraid to have him in their land, for they knew the Romans would not like it. So he was hunted down and at last took poison that he might not fall into the hands of the Romans (183).

Effects of the War

This war between the Romans and Hannibal was one of the greatest wars the world had ever seen. It was a war between a great man and a great nation. The Romans won because they were strong enough to live through the war. Hannibal thought that the Italians would all be on his side, but when he found that the best of them remained loyal to the Romans, he began to lose in strength. Though the Romans had the enemy for sixteen years in Italy, they could still send armies elsewhere; but the Carthaginians soon had to give way when the enemy landed in their country.

This war had two important effects on Rome:

➤ It made her the chief state of all the states along the Mediterranean Sea. She had begun the war to defend herself, but at its close she had conquered Carthage and had won Spain. She became, also, a great naval power and mistress of the Mediterranean, which was henceforth to be her road to conquest.

➤ When Hannibal had left Italy, Rome was very cruel to the Italian cities which had joined him. She no longer treated them kindly but made them her subjects. All except the Latins were harshly treated, and even the Latins soon had complaints to make against Rome. This fierce war had made the Romans more cruel. Also it had driven the people who lived on their farms in the country into the towns, and never afterwards do you find so many farmers in Italy. We shall see how bad this was as we go on.

HOW ROME
CONQUERED THE EAST

State of the East

The end of the war with Hannibal left Rome the greatest state in the West; fifty years after that time she was the greatest state in the East also. The East had been conquered (334-323) by Alexander the Great, king of Macedonia in the north of Greece. He had conquered and ruled over Asia Minor, Persia, Syria, Egypt, and even parts of India. When he died, all these countries were divided among his generals, and when the Romans first had anything to do with the East, there were three great kingdoms:

➤ Macedonia, which ruled over the greater part of Greece.

➤ Syria, which ruled over Asia Minor, though there was there a number of small states.

➤ Egypt, which was very rich and traded a great deal from its capital, Alexandria.

Italy and the East

Conquest of Macedonia and Syria

The first of these with whom Rome went to war was Macedonia. When the Romans had conquered Hannibal, they found that Philip, king of Macedonia, was becoming too powerful, and so when Athens asked for help against him, Rome began the second Macedonian war (200). In 197 the Roman general Titus Quinctius Flamininus conquered Philip at Cynoscephale and made Greece free, as he called it; but this really meant that the Greek towns came under the power of Rome instead of being under that of Philip. It was not long before the second of these great eastern powers, Syria, was conquered by the Romans. Antiochus, king of Syria, was obliged in 190 to give up Asia Minor, and all the kingdoms of Asia Minor looked up to Rome as their head.

How Rome Ruled the East

By these wars Rome had conquered the kings of Macedonia and Syria and had taken away from them Greece and Asia Minor, but she had not taken Greece or Asia under her own rule. Rome was never in a hurry to govern the countries she conquered. She left weak kings instead of strong ones and many little kingdoms instead of one large one, and then these small kings had to do what Rome told them to do. One king went to war against another, till at last Rome put an end to them all without any trouble and governed these countries herself. The next years, from 190 to 133, show us Rome following this plan and finishing the conquests she had begun. Macedonia was made a Roman province in 148. In Asia Minor also the Romans favored the kingdom of Pergamum, which grew larger, and its king did what the Romans wanted. At last, in 133, King Attalus III died and left Pergamum to the Roman people in his will. So the Romans made Asia into a Roman province and governed it themselves.

Conquest of Spain

In some countries, however, the Romans found it hard to conquer the people entirely. Spain gave them a great deal of trouble. Among the Lusitani, who lived in what we now call Portugal, there rose a hero, called Viriathus, who led his countrymen against the Romans. He was only a shepherd when he began, but he won battle after battle, and the Lusitani made him their king. For many years he fought against the Romans and even forced them to make peace with him. But this did not last long, and in the end the Roman general, Quintus Caepio, bribed three of the friends of Viriathus to murder him while he was asleep. So, too, in the north of Spain the city of Numantia refused to open its gates to the Romans and fought against them for many years (141-133). At last the Romans had to send their greatest general, Scipio Aemilianus; and he could only take the city by digging a ditch all around it so that no one could go in or come out, till at last the Numantines almost died of hunger. Before they surrendered, the chief men killed themselves, and when the gates were opened a few only came out, and they were nearly starved to death. Numantia was taken in 133, and after this Spain was made into two Roman provinces.

Destruction of Carthage

But the country that Rome treated most harshly was Carthage. Rome was still afraid of Carthage and so tried to find a reason for attacking her. After the second Punic war, Rome had taken under her protection Massinissa, king of Numidia, which was the country next to Carthage. Massinissa went to war with Carthage, and the Romans took his part in 149. The Carthaginians knew they could not fight with Rome, and so they offered to give up everything. First Rome asked for three hundred boys of the noblest parents, who were to be kept at Rome, to make sure of their fathers' obedience. Then the Romans asked for all the arms of the Carthaginians, and these also were given up. Last of all the Roman consul said that the Carthaginians must pull their city down, and build it again ten miles from the sea coast. This would, of course, ruin a trading city, and so in fury the Carthaginians refused; they made haste to repair their walls, and made new arms. The women cut off their hair to make bow strings, and the city was made ready for a siege. The siege lasted for three years (149-146), and the fighting was severe on both sides. The general who took the city was Publius Scipio Aemilianus. He first built a stone wall across the harbor of Carthage so as to shut in their ships, but the Carthaginians dug a canal on the other side and sailed out. However, Scipio tried again and built a great wall as high as the wall of the city so as to shut out the Carthaginians from the harbor. Then they began to give way, and the Romans forced an entrance into the city; but still every house had to be taken by storm. The Romans entered one house from another by knocking down the walls, and there were desperate fights in the rooms. At last only a tenth part of the population was left to surrender; all the rest had been killed. Carthage was set on fire and burned almost to the ground, and the land of Carthage was made a Roman province under the name of Africa.

Rome's Position in B.C. 133

Thus you see that in the year 133 Rome, besides ruling Italy, was ruler also of Macedonia, Greece, Asia, Spain, and Africa, in fact all of the countries around the Mediterranean Sea, which thus became a Roman lake. Also these were all the countries which at that time were *civilized*, that is, had made themselves into regular states, whose citizens lived together for their common good and built cities and made and obeyed laws. You see, then, how important the position of Rome was after these wars; she was the head of the civilized world. Some of the countries which Rome conquered were made into provinces and so were ruled by Roman governors. Others were still ruled over by their own kings or governors but had to do whatever Rome told them, and were really worse off than if they had been subjects.

Rome's Wars after B.C. 133

The wars Rome carried on after this time were against *uncivilized* peoples, that is, against peoples who did not yet live in cities, but were small tribes, which only helped one another when they were afraid of a great common danger, and which had no laws in common. Against these people Rome fought as a civilizing power. When she conquered them, she taught them to live together and obey laws. In this way the history of the nations of northern Europe begins with the account of their conquest by Rome.

HOW THE ROMANS
BEHAVED AS CONQUERORS

Change in the Character of the Romans

The Romans themselves were greatly changed by making all these conquests. Their great men were no longer simple farmers who left the plough to fight for their country and went back again when the enemy had been driven away. The Roman generals were now very rich men, who spent all their time in war or in the business of the state. They were no longer simple men doing their duty to their country, but they became proud and desired honors and wanted to be rich. No longer were the presents of foreign kings refused at Rome, but Roman generals asked for money wherever they went.

Influence of the Greeks

Of course, when the Romans conquered Greece and the East, they saw a great many things which they had never seen before; and they began to care more about eating and drinking and building fine houses. The Greeks were much cleverer than the Romans, or indeed than any people of the time, for all the best books and statues and pictures of the old world had been made by the Greek writers and artists. So the Romans not only learned many new things from the Greeks but gave up a great many of their own early beliefs. They thought less of their own Roman gods and no longer were as simple or as good as they had been before.

Publius Scipio Africanus

The man who was most fond of the Greeks and lived most like them was Publius Scipio Africanus. He was called Africanus after he had defeated Hannibal in Africa. Men in Rome were not fond of Publius Scipio, though he was a great general. They said he thought too much of himself and wished to do as he liked and did not behave like a Roman. His great enemy was Marcus Cato, who was a rough old man who did not like the new Greek fashions. At last a charge was brought against Lucius Scipio Asiaticus, who was the brother of Publius and had defeated Antiochus in Asia. He was accused of having taken for himself, as general, some money that belonged to the Roman people. Then Publius rose to speak for his brother, he took the account-books and tore them to pieces before the people and said: "Today fourteen years ago I defeated Hannibal at Zama; let us go and give thanks to the gods for saving the state." Then he and all the people went up to the Capitol, and his accusers were left alone. But after this he left Rome and died in exile, and the words "Ungrateful country" were written on his grave.

Marcus Cato

His enemy, Marcus Cato, tried to keep up the old Roman manners. He lived very simply and spent very little money. He took great pains in educating his children and making them strong in body. He always spoke against the bad habits which the Romans were learning, and when he was made censor, he punished many great men for things they had done. But though the Roman people listened to him and laughed at his sharp sayings and found much truth in them, still they did not try to make themselves any better.

The Roman Nobles

Let us try and see how the Roman people changed, now that they had become so great a nation.

You will remember that in the year 300 the old quarrels of the patricians and plebeians came to an end, and all were equal in the state. But very soon a new difference grew up among them. The rich plebeians and the chief patricians were the only people who were elected consuls. So a few families, whose members were generally elected magistrates, gradually separated themselves from the other families, and were called *optimates*, or nobles. These families thought themselves much better than the rest because they were richer and because they held the offices of state; and thus you see a new nobility, which was founded on money, grew up in Rome. Only rich men ever got into the Senate, and all the magistrates were chosen out of these noble families. These nobles agreed among themselves, and because they made up the Senate, they governed Rome as they pleased.

New Government of the Roman State

In former times the consuls had governed Rome with the help of the Senate; but now the Senate governed, and the consuls had to do what the Senate told them to do. At first the Senate governed very well, especially during the war with Hannibal; but after the wars in Asia everyone wanted to grow rich, and then the Senate tried to get money rather than to govern well. So all sorts of evils arose in Rome, and no one could prevent them. Though Rome was very powerful, still her greatest men were afraid. Cato asked sadly, "What will become of Rome when she has no longer any state to fear?" Scipio Aemilianus, who took Carthage, instead of praying as the magistrates always did, that the gods would *increase* the state, could only pray that the gods would *preserve* it.

You must see what these dangers were of which these great men were afraid. Perhaps this may be done most easily if you see what the government of the Senate did for Rome, for Italy, and for the Provinces.

What the New State of Things Did for Rome

Rome, you must remember, was a city, and so, when Rome grew great, the people of one city had to govern almost all the world. The people of the city were divided into the rich nobles and senators, the knights, and the common people. The nobles and senators took care of the government, as we have seen, but laws had to be made before the Assemblies of the people, and so the Senate had to please the people if it wanted to have its own way. The knights were the rich traders. They were called *knights* because in the old army of Rome all the richest men had to fight on horseback. Of course, in the new state of things

these knights very seldom went to the wars, but stayed at
Rome and did their business, and the Senate let them
gather the taxes in the provinces, so that they grew richer
and richer. The common people also had to be fed and
amused by the nobles, that they might be kept quiet and
contented. The magistrates in the provinces used to send
presents of grain to Rome, which were divided among the
people without their paying for it. Also every man before
he was elected a magistrate had to give great games for
the people's amusement in the Circus Maximus. The
Romans were always a cruel people, and their games were
cruel too. They had of course horse races and foot races;
but they also liked to see strange animals, such as lions
and tigers, brought to Rome and hunted to death in their
presence. The sport, however, of which they were most
fond were the gladiatorial fights, when men fought with
one another and killed one another for the amusement of
the people. Often these *gladiators* were prisoners taken in
war, but there was a number of men regularly trained to
this as a trade. Now, all these games were paid for by the
rich so as to please the people, and the games and gifts of
grain together attracted more and more people to come,
and so its poor people ceased to be really Romans and
became more and more a mob of idle and worthless folk.
But all the rule of the world was still in their hands.

Thus you see in Rome itself the Senate wanted to keep
all the power to itself; the knights wanted to grow rich
and would do anything to get money; the people were
lazy and only wanted to be fed and amused without
doing anything.

What the New State of Things Did for Italy

Italy had been ravaged by the war with Hannibal, and afterwards by the Romans when they punished those who had taken Hannibal's side. The little farms had been ruined, and men went to live in towns instead of living in the country. Every Roman when he grew rich wanted to have a great deal of land; so land grew too dear for the small farmer to buy, and large farms took the place of small ones. This land, which the Roman nobles thus got, was not generally rented out but was tilled by slaves. The Romans in their wars had made a great number of slaves; so to buy and use slaves was cheaper than to hire free laborers, and slaves were almost always used in Italy. A poor man could very seldom get work to do as a farm laborer, but had to go and live idly in a town or else become a soldier. Bands of slaves, chained together, did all the work in the fields.

You see, then, that the class of soldiers who had fought Rome's battles so well in her early days, the small farmers, had been ruined by the growth of wealth. Rome might become richer but would never be so strong again.

Another thing was that Rome, after driving Hannibal out of Italy, treated the Italians much more harshly than before. The Italians were looked upon as subjects, almost as much as the foreign peoples which Rome had been conquering. Even the Latins, who had been so faithful to Rome, were not rewarded; Rome no longer treated them as equals, but took from them by her harshness all the hopes they had had before of being some day made Roman citizens.

So Rome's government was not much liked in Italy itself.

Condition of the Provinces

The provinces were governed by magistrates sent every year from Rome by the Senate. The custom was that after a man had been consul in Rome, he should go and rule a province for a year. A man only became consul after he had held other magistracies, and to all of these he was elected by the people. He had, then, to make sure of his elections by giving very splendid games to the people, and these cost him a great deal of money. The governor of a Roman province generally left Rome very much in debt. He had during his year of office to make three large fortunes, one to pay his debts, one for himself to live upon, and one to bribe his judges if he were brought to trial. Of course, this money had to be gotten from the poor people whom he governed. If he did anything wrong and the people of the province complained to the Senate, the governor was brought to trial, but he was almost always acquitted. He bribed his judges, and the senators all hoped to go as governors of provinces some day, and so they would not be hard upon one another.

So the people of the provinces were sadly oppressed by this government of the Senate.

ATTEMPTS AT REFORM
BY THE GRACCHI

Dangers of the Roman State

You see how many dangers there were in the Roman state, and you see why Cato and Scipio feared about the future of Rome.

Before trying to see how these evils were to be gotten rid of, let us clearly say what they were:

➤ The Roman people were becoming a rabble, at the head of which was a small body of rich and selfish nobles, who fed and amused this rabble to make it do as they told it.

➤ Slave labor had taken the place of free labor in Italy, and the number of freemen was becoming smaller and smaller.

➤ Rome was treating the Italians harshl, and the Latins arrogantly, because the rabble of Rome did not want to give anyone else the privileges which they had themselves.

➤ The people of the provinces were everywhere oppressed.

Plans of Tiberius Gracchus for Reform

Now, in the year 133 an attempt was made in Rome to mend some of these evils. Tiberius Sempronius Gracchus was a Roman noble who had seen the sad state of Italy and who had been at the wars in Spain, and knew how badly the Romans treated the Spaniards, and how weak the Roman army really was.

So he came back to Rome to see whether he could not make things better. He got himself elected tribune of the plebs in 134, and at once proposed an Agrarian Law. The public land of Rome was now very large, and it was used by the nobles who paid no rent to the state for it. Tiberius Gracchus wanted to take this land and divide it into small farms for the poor people. Of course, the rich men did not like this, and as there were ten tribunes, they got one of the other tribunes to object to the law which Tiberius Gracchus brought forward. Now, no law could pass which a tribune objected to. But Tiberius Gracchus proposed to the people to turn this tribune out of his office, and so carry the law. The people agreed to do this, and the law was passed, but you see that the old laws of the state were broken to pass it. This was not a very good sign for the future; for if changes could not be made in Rome without breaking the laws, it seemed likely that the changes would do more harm than good.

Tiberius Gracchus soon found that this was the case. His law was very hard to carry out and did not do much for the poor people at once. The nobles hated him for it, and he knew that if he were not made tribune next year, the nobles would kill him. So he tried very hard to be made tribune, and the nobles tried to prevent him, and so there was a riot, in which Tiberius Gracchus and three hundred of his followers were killed. This was in the year 133 and was the beginning of a time of *revolution* in Rome, that is, a time in which neither side cared for the old laws, but both sides were ready to carry what they wanted by force and bloodshed if they could not do it in any other way.

Reforms of Gaius Gracchus

Ten years after the death of Tiberius Cracchus, his younger brother, Gaius Sempronius Gracchus, tried to carry out the same plans (123). It was in vain that his mother strove to prevent him. She had been very proud of her sons when they were boys, and once when a Roman lady was showing her all sorts of fine jewels, Cornelia (for that was her name) called for her sons, and when they came she put her arms around them and said, "These are my jewels." Now one of them had been killed as a rebel, and she was afraid that the other might soon be killed also.

Gaius Gracchus went much farther than his brother. He seems to have wished to break up the government altogether. He was tribune and carried laws by going to the people at once without paying any attention to the consuls or Senate. He wanted to overthrow the government of the nobles and make a government of the people with himself at its head. First he won over the people by passing a law that they should always have grain sold them at a very low price. Then he won over the knights to side with him against the nobles by giving them greater chances of making money in the provinces, and also by ordering that the jurymen for the future should be chosen from the knights and not from the Senate. In this way the knights had all the power of the law-courts on their side and now were quite

equal to the Senate. The rich men had before this joined
with the nobles, but now the rich men and the nobles were
opposed to one another. Gaius Gracchus said that he had
thrown down a dagger for the enemies of the people to stab
one another with.

How Gaius Gracchus Failed

When Gaius Gracchus had thus gotten the people and
the knights on his side, he passed an Agrarian Law, and
founded many colonies for the poor people both in Italy
and outside Italy. As long as he only tried to do good to the
people of Rome, they were very pleased with all he did. But
in his second tribunate (122), he proposed to make all the
Latins citizens of Rome and to give all the Italians the rights
which the Latins then had. The Romans, however, did not
like this; they thought that it was better to keep to themselves their favorable position, which meant their cheap
bread and their games, and so they opposed this law of
Gracchus. It was a great pity that they opposed it, as it
would have done a great deal of good to the Roman state.
For it was impossible for the people of one city to govern
the whole world unless they were ready to take into their
city everyone who was fit to obey their laws. Now the
Latins were almost the same people as the Romans and had
always been their allies and had obeyed Rome's laws and
fought bravely for her. If the city of Rome was to grow larger, it could not have any new citizens better than the Latins.
If the city of Rome was not to grow larger, it would have to
govern all its subjects by force, and it would be impossible
for the few people of one city to govern the world by force
only. You will see how this difficulty came back again, and
the Romans had to give way at last; but it would have
saved them much misery if they had been wise enough to

take the Latins into the state of their own accord, as Gaius Gracchus wanted them to do. Next year, 121, Gaius Gracchus was not made tribune. He tried to live quietly in Rome, but soon there was a riot in which the nobles attacked him and his followers. Many were killed, and Gaius Gracchus among them.

You see from this what a bad condition Rome was in, and how different it was now from the old times of the struggles between the patricians and plebeians. Then the Romans upheld the laws and did not kill one another, but now the laws were thought very little of, and force and self-ishness seemed to do everything.

TIME OF MISGOVERNMENT
AT ROME

Slave War in Sicily

After the death of Gaius Gracchus the nobles did what they pleased in Rome. They paid no more attention to the Agrarian Law, and the state of Italy grew worse and worse. The slaves were so numerous that it was very hard to keep them under control. In Sicily there was a great war carried on by runaway slaves, who made themselves into an army, and for five years resisted the Romans (104-99).

War with Jugurtha

The nobles cared nothing for Rome's honor, but only for their own pockets. They governed badly and took bribes from foreign kings, who were allowed to do what they liked if they could pay enough. This was especially seen in a war that took place in Africa. After Carthage had been destroyed, the greatest state in Africa was Numidia. The king of Numidia was a friend of the Roman people and had fought with them against Carthage. So Rome had a good deal to do with Numidia, and the Numidians often helped Rome in her wars. In 118 a king of Numidia died and left the kingdom to his two sons and an adopted son named Jugurtha. Jugurtha determined to have the kingdom all to himself, and so he murdered one of the sons and made war upon the other, who applied to Rome for help. The Senate was bribed by Jugurtha and did all it could to please him; at last, however, Jugurtha besieged his brother in Cirta, and when he took the city put him and all his army to death (112). After this the Romans thought they must interfere, but the Senate for more money was willing to let Jugurtha off very easily. He came to Rome to excuse himself before the people, and while he was there he had a Numidian prince, of whom he was afraid, murdered in Rome itself. But his bribes were stronger than the laws, and when he left Rome he looked back upon it and said, "Oh city, where everything is sold, you would sell yourself if you could only find a buyer."

The Romans declared war against Jugurtha, but he bribed the generals, and for three years very little was done against him. At last, in 108, a good general who would not take bribes, Quintus Metellus, went against him and defeated him. Metellus would have finished the war, but in 106 the command was taken from him by Gaius Marius the consul

Rise of Gaius Marius

This Gaius Marius was a man of low birth but a good soldier. He had risen in war by his bravery and had held magistracies in Rome. He was an officer in the army of

Metellus and was very much liked by the common soldiers, for he was a rough man like themselves, and talked with them, and lived as they did. It is said that Metellus laughed at him because of his low birth, and so Marius disliked him. Also in Africa a soothsayer told Marius that he would become a very great man, greater than he ever had hoped to be. So Marius left Africa and went to Rome to try to be elected consul in l06. He found fault with Metellus before the people and said that he could carry on the war better himself. So the people elected him consul, and more than that, they said that he should be general in Africa instead of Metellus. Before this time the Senate always said what the consuls should do; but since the time of the Gracchi the assemblies of the people had done more and more of the business of the state.

Marius finished the war in Africa and brought Jugurtha in triumph to Italy in 104. But you see this war ought never to have taken place if the Senate had governed honestly; and when it did take place, it ought to have been finished much sooner if the generals had conducted it honestly. However, when it was over, Marius was the most powerful man in Rome. He was the leader of the popular party and also the general of the army.

Power of the Army at Rome

The army had greatly changed since the time of Hannibal. The Roman soldiers were no longer citizens who fought when their country wanted them, and then went back to their work. But as wars were now constantly going on, and going on too in distant countries, this could no longer be the case, and the army was full of men who took to a soldier's life as a career. Marius was the favorite of these soldiers; he was a career soldier by trade himself and had risen in consequence to power in the state. Notice, then, that when Marius was elected consul, it was a sign that the government for the future was to be carried on by the army, as well as by the people and the nobles.

Wars against the Teutones and Cimbri

Marius was soon needed to carry on another war. Two great tribes of barbarians from the North had entered Gaul west of the Alps and threatened to drive out the Romans and even attack Italy. They came with their wives and children, like a wandering people looking for a home. They seemed very strange to the Romans, these people with blue eyes and blond hair. They fought bravely in battle, rushing upon their enemy with fury. At first these Cimbri defeated the Roman generals in southern Gaul, where the Romans had conquered the country along the Rhone, and made it a province, which is still called the province, or *Provence.* The Romans, after this defeat, were afraid of another burning of their city by barbarians, and so Marius was elected consul again, and for the next five years he was elected again and again. This was against the custom and had never been done to anyone before. It shows how great the fear of the Romans must have been and how powerful Marius had become. In the year 102 the Teutones and the Cimbri marched to attack Italy, but Marius defeated them in two great battles. Afterwards when he went back to Rome in triumph he was so powerful that he could have done what he chose in the state. The people were very grateful to him, the soldiers were very fond of him, and the nobles were very much afraid of him.

Marius in Rome

But Marius did not think much of the good of the state:; he thought much more of his own greatness and how he might become a still greater man. So, first, he joined the party of the people, and one of the tribunes, Lucius Appuleius Saturninus, brought forward some laws like those of Gaius Gracchus, and Marius helped him. But there were riots in consequence, and the Senate begged Marius to help them in putting down the riots. For a time Marius hesitated about what to do, but at last he armed the people, and Saturninus was killed (99). But now neither side liked Marius, for he was true to neither and did only what he thought would make himself most powerful. So for the future Marius was not likely to be of much use in the troubles of the Roman state.

Marcus Livius Drusus

These troubles began rapidly to increase; for the Italians were growing more and more angry at the way in which Rome treated them. The Latins also had been ordered to leave Rome, where many of them used to live, because some of the nobles thought they voted against them in the Assemblies of the people. To prevent these grievances from breaking out into war, Marcus Livius Drusus, a tribune, proposed in 91 that the citizenship of Rome should be given to all the Italians, and so all the Italians would be made equal with the people who lived in Rome. But both nobles and people were very angry with Drusus for bringing forward this law, and on the day on which it was to have been voted upon Drusus was murdered. He was stabbed as he was going into his house, and died saying, "When will the state have another citizen like me."

War with the Italians

The news of this murder stirred up the Italians at once to rebel. They saw that Rome would never of her own accord give them any rights, and so they tried to get them by force. The chief of the rebel peoples were the Samnites. In the year 90 began a war in which Italy was divided into two parts, and one fought against the other. At the end of the first year's war the Romans felt that they must give way. But they gave way little by little; at first they gave Roman citizenship to all the Italians who had not yet revolted; then to all who should lay down their arms in two months. In this way Rome won back all who were not very hostile to her, and so could go against Samnium, which had shown again all the old vigor of the Samnite wars.

In this war there arose a new general among the Romans, Lucius Cornelius Sulla. He was a noble who had first learned war under Marius when he fought against Jugurtha. But he had not shown himself very desirous of holding office in the state and had not put himself forward. In the year 89 he was commander against the Samnites and defeated them.

Results of the Social War

At the end of the year 89 all the peoples of Italy except the Samnites and Lucanians had submitted to Rome and had received Roman citizenship. This war, which is called the *Social* War, or war *against the allies,* was almost over. Rome had had to give way and had been forced to go back to her old plan of making other people equal with herself and always from time to time taking in fresh citizens into the state. This plan had for a time been laid aside by the nobles, and Rome had in consequence run into great danger. This war had destroyed houses and wasted fields in Italy almost as much as the war with Hannibal had done. It made the number of farms in Italy smaller than it had been before and drove more men who before would have been farmers to become soldiers.

Causes of the Civil Wars

You find, then, Rome's armies growing larger and larger, and the men who went to be soldiers were better than the men who stayed at Rome and idled, and were fed by the Senate, and spent all their time in baths and sports in the Circus Maximus. You see, then, that the army was becoming more important than the people, and the generals of the army were becoming more powerful than the magistrates of the state. When this was the case, it was plain that questions about government would no longer be agreed upon, but be fought about. This was what happened: the government could not do anything against the generals of the army. For the next fifty years we have a period of Civil War.

THE CIVIL WARS
OF ROME

War with Mithridates

This Social War was not the only difficulty which the Senate had before them. During the last twenty years a great power had been forming in the East under Mithridates, king of Pontus. Pontus is in the northeast of Asia Minor, next to Armenia. Mithridates for some time went on conquering the people in his neighborhood, and when the Romans interfered he stopped for a little while and then went on again. At last, war broke out with Rome in the year 88, when Lucius Cornelius Sulla was one of the consuls. He was appointed by the Senate to carry on the war.

Marius and Sulla

But Marius, though old, wanted the command for himself, and so he joined with one of the tribunes, P. Sulpicius Rufus, who brought before the people a number of laws which went against the Senate, and among them a law that Marius should be appointed general in the East instead of Sulla. When Sulla's soldiers heard this, they were very angry, marched against Rome, drove out Marius, and put Sulpicius to death. It was the first time that Rome had been taken by her own army, but it was not to be the last. From this time on the chief power in Rome had to be fought for, and Rome had to pay those who fought. Sulla did not stay long in Rome, but he passed some laws to make the Senate stronger and the tribunes weaker. Then, hoping things would remain quiet at home, he went off to the war against Mithridates.

Sulla in the East

It was quite time that he did so, as Mithridates had entered Asia Minor and had ordered all the Italians there to be put to death; 150,000 are said to have been killed. He had also sent troops into Greece, which had rebelled against the Romans and had joined him. So when Sulla landed in Greece in 87, he had quite enough to do. He managed, however, to win back Greece, and meanwhile Mithridates made himself unpopular in Asia Minor; so that when another army was sent from Rome, which landed in Asia, Mithridates was obliged to ask for peace in 84. Sulla made peace because he wanted to go back to Italy, where things again were in confusion.

Marius in Exile

After Sulla had left Rome the two consuls began to quarrel, one being on the side of Sulla, the other on the side of Marius. At last L. Cornelius Cinna, who was Marius' consul, gathered an army and brought Marius back. Marius had had many troubles in trying to escape from Italy. The sailors of a ship on which he wished to go to Africa persuaded him to land near Minturnae, and then sailed away and left him. He was pursued and taken prisoner, though he had tried to hide himself by standing up to the chin in a marsh. He was put in prison at Minturnae, and the magistrates sent a Gallic slave to put him to death in prison; but when the slave came to Marius the old man's eyes flashed so terribly through the dark prison as he said, "Fellow, darest thou kill Gaius Marius?" that the man dropped his sword and ran away. Then the magistrates were ashamed, and let Marius go. He crossed over to Africa, but had no sooner landed than he was warned by the magistrates to go away. Those who were sent to tell him to go found him sitting among the ruins of Carthage, and when they had given their message he said, "Say you have seen Gaius Marius among the ruins of Carthage."

Cinna and Sulla

Now that his troubles were over, Marius came back to Rome very savage after all that he had suffered. He and Cinna put to death all the chief people who were opposed to them. For five days the gates of Rome were shut, and Marius went through the streets with a body of soldiers, who put to death anyone he pointed out. In the year 86 Marius was made consul for the seventh time, but he did not live long to enjoy his power. He died at the age of seventy-one, hated by all for his cruelty.

Cinna continued to hold the chief power at Rome till 84, when Sulla, who had finished the war with Mithridates for the present, prepared to cross to Italy. Cinna thought it better to go and meet him in the East,—but he was murdered at Ancona by his troops as he was on the point of setting out. When Sulla landed in Italy he had only 40,000 men, while the consuls had 100,000. He could not therefore march to Rome at once, so he remained in southern Italy and won over the people by kindness, defeating the armies sent against him.

Sulla's Victory

In the year 82 the struggle became more important. The Samnites, who had not yet been subdued after the Social War, joined with the old party of Marius. Sulla was making good his position on every side, and at last in despair the Samnites and Marians retreated to Rome and would have destroyed it. But Sulla followed them, and a great battle was fought just outside the walls of Rome. The Samnites were with difficulty defeated, and Rome was saved.

So Sulla was now master of Rome and could do there what he liked. You see how in all these last five years the power had been in the hands of one man, and the Senate and all the old ways of governing had been set aside. Now Sulla decided to do all that could be done to bring back these old ways and to set up the government of the nobility again.

Sulla's Government

Sulla showed quite as much cruelty as Marius had done. He seems to have wished to make his government quiet and peaceable by putting to death everybody who was opposed to it. Lists were put out every day of men who were outlawed, and whom anyone might put to death without trial, and also get paid for doing it. It is said that 4,700 of the chief people in Rome were killed in this way, and all their property was sold for the good of the state.

This was a terrible way of bringing in peaceful government and was hardly likely to succeed. You may think how bad an effect it had on the morals of those who lived through it. Many men suddenly became rich; many more hoped that they would gain something for themselves by killing others. Everyone was made anxious and unquiet for a long while to come.

Then, when Sulla had gotten rid of all his enemies, he went on to put the government in order. He was made dictator, and as such passed a number of laws to make the Senate stronger. When he had done this, he had himself elected consul (80) to show how a consul ought to govern. He gave most magnificent games and fed all the people of Rome for many days. Then he retired from Rome and from its politics to a house in the country, where he died in 78, and was honored with the grandest funeral that had ever been seen in Rome.

Troubles after Sulla's Death

It might have seemed that Rome would now go on quietly, but the old evils soon broke out again. The Social War, and the Civil War which followed, had wasted Italy and reduced its population still more than before. It is true that Sulla, when his wars were over, had given his soldiers farms in Italy by founding what were called *military colonies.* But these soldiers were restless and soon sold their land and went to live in the towns, and so Italy again went back to large farms tilled by slaves.

Again, the Senate and the nobility, on being restored to power by Sulla, looked upon the state as something they had a right to use for their own purposes. They were more bent upon making money than ever, and many of them made larger fortunes than ever. Their government was selfish at home and weak abroad, so it pleased nobody and soon found troubles on every side.

War with Sertorius in Spain

First, in Spain, there was a rebellion against Rome started by a Roman, Quintus Sertorius. He had been a general on the side of Marius, and fled to Spain when Sulla conquered. There he gathered the Spaniards around him, and also a large number of Romans who had fled like himself. He had the power of getting barbarous people to obey him, and so he lived among the Spaniards and taught them all the virtues of Rome. For many years the Romans could do nothing against him. They sent their best general, Gnaeus Pompeius, but he did not do very much. At last the Spaniards became tired of the long war and the misery it brought. Many deserted Sertorius, and he became suspicious of the rest. Then some of his officers made a plot against him and murdered him in his tent at supper (72). After his death the rebellion was put down, and Spain again became obedient.

Troubles in the East

But there were other troubles quite as great for the Romans. The Mediterranean Sea swarmed with pirates who disturbed all the Roman trade. Mithridates, too, in Pontus, had only been waiting to gather his forces together, and in the year 74 he again went to war with the Romans. At first he was beaten by the Roman general, Lucullus, and driven from his kingdom, but he got help from the king of Armenia, and in the year 67 Lucullus was defeated, and Mithridates returned to Pontus. So far the Romans had gained nothing by the war. At the same time, also, the

Roman fleet had failed in its attempts against the pirates in
the Mediterranean.

Rebellion of the Gladiators

All these things showed how unable the Senate was to
carry on the government in matters abroad. Their weakness
at home was shown at the same time by a dreadful war
which again laid waste Italy. This was the *Gladiatorial War*
which broke out in 73. The *gladiators* were men who were
trained to fight with one another and kill one another to
amuse the Roman people at their games. These men were
regularly taught their horrible trade, and there were
schools of gladiators in different parts of Italy. Many of
them were prisoners who had been taken in battle against
the Romans and were now being taught how to amuse their
conquerors by their death. A number of these gladiators
made their escape from a prison at Capua under a brave
leader called Spartacus. Their numbers grew very quickly,
for slaves and gladiators escaped on every side, and the
army of Spartacus soon reached 40,000 men. The Roman
generals were defeated by them, and Rome was in great
danger of an attack. Spartacus himself was a great man and
wished to lead his followers over the Alps back to their
native land of Gaul or Germany. But they found they could
rob as they pleased in Italy, so they stayed there and did
almost what they liked; but they soon began to quarrel
among themselves, and at last, in the year 71, were defeated by the Roman general Marcus Crassus. At the same time
Gnaeus Pompeius, who had been sent for from Spain after
the death of Sertorius, fell upon the rest of the slave army
and almost entirely destroyed them.

Power of Gnaeus Pompeius

Many people now expected that Pompey would behave like Sulla, enter Rome with his army, and so put himself at the head of the government. But he came back quietly, and he and Crassus were elected consuls for the year 70. From this time on Pompey was the most important man in Rome. He tried to please both the party of the nobles and the party of the people. It seemed to the people that he was the only man who could put an end to the wars in which they were engaged; so, in 67, he was made general against the pirates by a special decree of the people. In three months he cleared the Mediterranean Sea of pirates, pursued them to Cilicia, and destroyed their strongholds.

Pompey in the East

Meanwhile Mithridates had been making gains in Asia, and the general sent by the Senate had shown himself quite useless. So, at the proposal of one of the tribunes, the command in Asia was given to Pompey. The Senate opposed this, but in vain. The people were too strong for them, and the Senate found that the favorite of the people could do anything he pleased.

Pompey , therefore, went against Mithridates in 66. He drove him out of his kingdom of Pontus and followed him into Armenia, whither he fled. For a time Mithridates still tried to resist, but at last his own son rebelled against him, and Mithridates in the year 63 killed himself that he might not be given over to the Romans. After this Pompey went on to Syria, which he brought under the rule of Rome. From Syria he passed to Judaea, which for a time resisted; and even after Jerusalem had surrendered, a few Jews still held out on the Temple rock; but they were at last surprised on the Sabbath, since they did not think it right to fight on that day. Pompey entered the Temple, and was amazed at seeing no idol or statue in it, for the Romans did not understand the religion of the Jews. After this Pontus, Cilicia, Syria, and Crete were all made provinces of Rome, and in the year 61 Pompey came back to Rome again a successful conqueror.

Troubles in Rome

But while Pompey had been establishing order abroad, the government of the Senate had become still weaker in Rome itself. Ever since the time of the Gracchi there had been a party of the people opposed to the nobles and the Senate.

He saw how little good this party had gotten from the help of Marius and his troops. Sulla had put it down for a time and had given the power back again to the Senate. But in these last few years the Senate had been growing weaker, and the party of the people had been growing stronger. Pompey had been a friend of Sulla's, and so belonged to the nobles' party, but the nobles were rather afraid of him, and he did not trust them.

Chief Men in Rome

The best man among the nobles was Marcus Porcius Cato, who kept to the old Roman virtues and wished to keep also to the old Roman government. Another man of great consequence in Rome was Marcus Licinius Crassus, who had made a very large fortune, which he was always increasing. He tried to please both parties and so get everything he could for himself. Marcus Tullius Cicero was also a great man in Rome. He was not of old family or very rich, but he rose by his own talents and especially by his great power of speaking to men so as to persuade them. He was one of the greatest *orators,* or *public speakers,* that there has ever been, and we still have many of his speeches to the Roman people which tell us a great deal about these times. He was a moderate man who wished to keep Rome at peace and also to put an end to the chief abuses which he saw. He wished to reform the old plan of government by the Senate, but he did not wish to change it. The great leader of the popular party was Gaius Julius Caesar; he was of a noble family, but Marius had married his aunt, and he himself had married Cinna's daughter, and so he was very much liked by the people. He was resolved to destroy the government of the Senate and then rule Rome himself in the name of the people. But as yet he had no army, and so he was waiting in Rome to see how he could get one in due time.

Conspiracy of Catiline

How dangerous the state of things was in Rome may be seen from the conspiracy of Lucius Sergius Catilina. He was a noble and had been a friend of Sulla's, but had run into debt and was now the leader of a band of young nobles who were all ruined, and who hoped to get more money if they could violently overthrow the government. Catiline joined the party of the people and tried to be elected consul while Pompey was away; but in the year 63 he was not elected, while Cicero was. Catiline is said by Cicero to have intended to murder him, and then to rise and burn the city and rob as he and his followers pleased. Though the Senate believed this, yet they were afraid to take Catiline prisoner. He left Rome and raised an army, whereupon his friends in

Rome were put to death by Cicero's orders. Next year Catiline was killed in a battle against the Senate's army, and his troops were all scattered. You see how little feeling there was in Rome for law and order, when a man was suspected of standing for the consulship that he might use his office as a means of plundering Rome. People did not know whether Catiline's plans were lawful or unlawful. And afterwards Cicero was exiled for putting Catiline's followers to death without trial. This shows you how hard it was for a magistrate to know what to do in Rome, and how party feeling decided everything, and there was very little care for the good of the state.

Pompey, Caesar, and Crassus

This was the state of things when Pompey returned in 61. It was again thought that he would bring his army into Rome and so rule the Senate. But he did not, and came back to Rome as a simple citizen (61). He found, however, that when the first gratitude was over he was not so powerful as he expected to be. Gradually he quarreled about many little matters with the Senate. Caesar saw this and took advantage of it. He agreed with Pompey and Crassus that they should all three work together to get what they each wanted. In the year 59 Caesar was elected consul, and as such passed an Agrarian law which was to give lands to Pompey's veterans. Then a law was passed by the people making Caesar the governor of Gaul for five years and putting him at the head of a large army.

Caesar had now gotten what he wanted: he had gotten the opportunity of showing himself to be a great general, and so of gaining popularity with the Roman people. He could now make himself the equal of Pompey and hoped soon to become a greater man than he was. Above all, he could train an army attached to him and ready to do whatever he told it.

Caesar in Gaul

So in the year 58 Caesar went off to Gaul, where he soon found plenty to do. In the next seven years he succeeded in entirely conquering all the land north of the Pyrenees and west of the Rhine. He even crossed over to Britain (54), and, though he did not stay to conquer it, he first brought the Romans into the land where the English live now, though the British alone lived there then. In Gaul Caesar showed what a very great man he was. He was busy in conquering Gaul, but he never lost sight of things in Rome at the same time. He was a skillful general and also a great writer as well, and has left us his own account of his wars in Gaul, where he was beloved both by the Roman soldiers and also by the natives of Gaul. He was kind to those that he conquered, yet he always took care that they should be thoroughly beaten. Caesar built roads in Gaul and brought in Roman ideas and Roman customs, and also taught all his officers to deal kindly with the Gauls. In this way he succeeded in making those of the Gauls who were not killed or made slaves quite content to be ruled by the Romans. Though he was only there ten years altogether, and when he left he took his army with him, still the Gauls did not rebel against Rome. This conquest of Gaul by Caesar is the greatest instance in Roman history of the way in which Rome could not only conquer, but could bind the conquered countries to herself. It was also most important for the future of Rome herself. You have seen how greatly the people of Italy were declining in numbers and in energy. The Gauls became children of Rome, and you will soon see that many of Rome's greatest men came from Gaul. Also this conquest of Gaul by Caesar first brought the power of Rome into those parts of Europe which our own history has most to do with. Caesar's invasion of Britain is the first great fact that we have related to us about this country.

Caesar's Influence in Rome

But Caesar had to keep a close watch all this while on things that were going on in Rome. He had been sent to Gaul first for five years. But he wanted to stay there longer to get more money and become better known to his soldiers; also, the hordes of slaves he had gotten made him rich enough to pay his debts in Rome and to buy over to his side many men who were powerful with the people. He could only stay in Gaul if Pompey and Crassus would help him, or at all events would not prevent it. In Rome itself there was great confusion. Every year the election to the consulship caused a war of parties. There were constant riots in the streets, and everyone was discontented. Pompey found that he was becoming less and less powerful with the Senate and also with the people.

Plans of Caesar, Pompey, and Crassus

Men looked to Caesar for advice, and in the year 56 Pompey and Crassus went to meet him at Luca. There they agreed to unite again, and get by their united influence all that each of them wanted. So in the next year, 55, Pompey and Crassus were elected consuls with the help of soldiers whom Caesar sent from his army in Gaul to vote in the assembly at Rome. As soon as they became consuls, they proposed to extend Caesar's command in Gaul for five years more. Then a tribune proposed to the people that the province of Syria should be given for five years to Crassus, and the province of Spain for five years to Pompey.

So these three men, Caesar, Pompey, and Crassus, divided all the power in Rome. The Senate could do nothing against them. The old Roman Republic was beginning to fall, and the power of the nobles, as a body, had given way before the wealth and influence of individuals.

Death of Crassus

Crassus went away to Syria at once, where he was killed in battle against the Parthians in the year 53. These Parthians were the great enemies of Rome in the East for some time to come; they lived among the deserts, where the Romans found it hard to follow them. This defeat of Crassus at Carrhae was a severe blow to the Roman power in the East. But, more than this, the death of Crassus broke the bond of union between Caesar and Pompey. There were now only two men, and not three, to share the power in Rome, and so Caesar and Pompey became rivals, with no one to stand between them.

Rivalry of Pompey and Caesar

Pompey had not gone to his province in Spain; he waited in Rome, which was not customary for the magistrate of a province. Also, he got the Senate to give him the province of Spain for five more years. By this means he became superior to Caesar, for when Caesar was to give up his province of Gaul and also his army, as he would have to do in the year 48, Pompey would still be governor of Spain and would have an army at his command. Caesar would have to come to Rome and live as a private noble, while Pompey would have all the power as general of an army. But meanwhile the constant riots in Rome gave more and more power to Pompey. The Senate could do very little to keep order, and Pompey hoped that, if he waited, things would become so bad that he would be called in to keep order, and so would get all the power for himself.

Caesar's friends of course did not like this, and Caesar was afraid that when he came back to Rome as a private man he would be brought to trial on some charge or another before the people, and then would be condemned by the votes of Pompey's soldiers. There was no certainty what might happen, and Caesar was determined to carry out his own plans and to alter the government of Rome. The Senate was more afraid of him than of Pompey, who made himself the head of the party of the nobles and those who favored the existing form of government. Caesar, on the other hand, was the leader of the common people and of those who wished for a reform in the government. It was soon very clear to everyone that the questions in dispute would never be settled peaceably, but that there would be a great civil war.

Quarrel of Pompey and Caesar

This was the question about which the war broke out: Caesar demanded that either both he and Pompey should give up their provinces at the same time, or he should be allowed to stand for the consulship while absent in Gaul so that he might come to Rome as consul and be as strong as Pompey in the state. Caesar was at the head of an army and had many friends in Rome, but the Senate did not know how strong he was, and so they refused his proposals, and when two of the tribunes took Caesar's side they were threatened with loss of their office. They fled to Caesar, who now had a cause for war, and who advanced into Roman ground, passing the little river Rubicon, which separates Gaul from Italy. He said he came to defend the tribunes of the people against the Senate. In January, 49, the great war broke out.

Civil War of Pompey and Caesar

Pompey was taken by surprise when Caesar actually came against him, and when he found that troops did not gather around him he left Rome with the consuls and Senate, and sailed to Greece. In sixty days Caesar had gained possession of Italy; but he only spent a few days in Rome and then hurried to Spain to fight Pompey's army there. In the battle of Ilerda he defeated Pompey's generals and broke up their army. Then he came back to Rome, and by his kindness and justice won over all those who did not care much how Rome was governed, but only wanted to live peaceably.

Defeat of Pompey

Next year (48) he crossed over to Greece, where Pompey had gathered a large army, and the great battle that was to decide the fate of Rome was fought on the Pharsalian plain. Pompey's army was twice as large as Caesar's, but Caesar's troops had fought with him in Gaul, and he knew he could trust them. It is said that he gave an order to his men before the battle to strike at the enemies' faces, for he knew that a wound in the face would frighten the Roman nobles. After a long battle, Caesar was victorious. Pompey did not stay to fight again, but fled to Egypt, where he was murdered in a boat as he was landing. Caesar, who followed after him, wept when Pompey's head was brought him. He used his victory very mercifully and did not put anyone to death, for he did not only want to conquer; he wanted his conquest to last, and he knew that he could only establish his own power on justice and mercy.

Caesar in the East

When Caesar followed Pompey to Egypt, he found there a quarrel going on about the kingdom between Ptolomy XII, a boy of fourteen, and his sister Cleopatra. Caesar took the side of Cleopatra and made her queen after Ptolomy had been killed in battle. Then he crossed over to Asia, where he defeated a rebel king at Zela, and wrote his famous letter to the Roman Senate "Veni, vidi, vici," (I came, I saw, I conquered). He had no sooner reached Rome than he set off again for Africa, where many of Pompey's party had assembled and were gathering troops among the Africans. They were defeated with great slaughter at Thapsus (46).

Caesar in Rome

Still Caesar could not rest, for the sons of Pompey had raised an army in Spain, where they were beaten by Caesar after a desperate battle at Munda (45). After that Caesar came back to Rome as master of the Roman world. The Senate made him dictator for life and gave him every possible honor that could be found. But Caesar wished to establish absolute power and to hand it on to others after him, so he wanted to be made king at once and change the whole form of the Roman government from a Republic to a Monarchy—but a Monarchy resting on the people. He wanted to take in among the number of the Roman citizens the people of the provinces as soon as they showed themselves ready for it. He wanted also to make the Senate a council of advisers to the king, and he wanted to bring into it not only Roman nobles, but also the chief men of the provinces.

Murder of Caesar

Now, many of the Romans disliked these changes and disliked Caesar. So, just as he was beginning to settle down in Rome to live quietly after all his hard work, a plot was formed against him. He was murdered in the Senate building (March 15, 44) by a band of men, among whom M. Junius Brutus and G. Cassius Longinus were the chief. They were all men to whom Caesar had shown great kindness, but they thought it was their duty to maintain the Roman state instead of submitting to a single master, and so they murdered Caesar in the name of liberty. Caesar died at the age of fifty-six, and is perhaps the greatest man in all history, when we consider both the greatness of the things he did and the wonderful powers of mind and body which he showed. He was not only a great general but also a great statesman and a great writer. He had many faults, for the times in which he lived were full of wickedness; but the poor people liked him, and his soldiers were entirely devoted to him.

Antonius and Octavian

The murder of Caesar, however, did not restore the old government of the Senate, as Brutus and Cassius thought it would do. It only brought on new disturbances and civil war for the next thirteen years. Caesar had left as his heir Gaius Octavius, his great-nephew, the son of his sister's daughter, but he was only a boy of eighteen at the time of

Caesar's death and was being educated in Greece. By Caesar's will he was adopted as his son, and so changed his name to Gaius Julius Caesar Octavianus. In Rome, however, was one of Caesar's generals, Marc Antony, who stirred up the people against Brutus and Cassius, so that they had to leave Rome. Then Caesar's old soldiers gathered round Antony and asked to avenge their leader's death. Antony hoped by means of this army to make himself master of Rome, as Caesar had done. But Octavian, young as he was, was wise and cautious. He came to Rome and made himself popular with everyone. Many of Caesar's old soldiers came to his support, and he soon became powerful. When war broke out between the Senate and Antony he sided with the Senate, till Antony was defeated in the battle of Mutina (43), where also the two consuls who were commanding for the Senate were killed. Then Octavian came to Rome with his troops and forced his own election as consul. Then, having gotten a position of real power, he made peace with Antony and with Marcus Lepidus, who, as governor of part of Spain and Gaul, had an army at his command.

Second Triumvirate

Thus was formed (43) what is known as the second *triumvirate* or *board of three men.* Just as, twelve years before, the affairs of Rome had been settled by three men, Pompey, Caesar, and Crassus, so now were they settled by three men who found themselves at the head of armies, Octavian, Antony, and Lepidus. The first thing they did was to secure themselves by putting everyone to death of whom any of the three was afraid, just as Sulla had done before. One of the people who was killed at this time was the great orator, Marcus Tullius Cicero. He had stood firmly by the Senate, and had spoken very fiercely against Antony in some very celebrated speeches, and so he was killed at the age of sixty-four.

When they had thus settled matters in Rome, they had to face Brutus and Cassius, who had gathered together a large army in Macedonia, while Sextus Pompey, the son of Gnaeus Pompeius, had collected a fleet and was in possession of Sicily. But Brutus and Cassius were not good generals and despaired too soon of their cause. In two battles fought at Philippi they were defeated (42); in the first battle Cassius committed suicide, and in the second Brutus did the same.

Octavian in Italy

After this battle Antony went to the East, where he met Cleopatra, the queen of Egypt, and became so fond of her that he stayed with her in Egypt. Octavian went back to Italy, where he tried to establish order. It was at last agreed that Antony should rule the East, Octavian the West, and Lepidus Africa. Octavian had the hardest work, as he had no ships, and Sextus Pompey, who had a large fleet, could prevent the grain ships from sailing to Rome, and so could produce famine. Octavian, therefore, had to get together a fleet of his own and also to try to keep the Romans quiet. At first his ships were defeated, and he was in great difficulties, but at last, in 36, he succeeded in overcoming Pompey, who was, however, joined by Lepidus, through fear of Octavian growing too powerful. Lepidus was defeated and deprived of his power, and Sextus Pompeius was driven to take refuge in the East, where he was put to death by Antony.

Civil War of Octavian and Antony

It was now Antony's turn to be afraid of the power of Octavian, who was master of Italy, which he had saved from great distress and where he had quietly and moderately introduced law and order. All Caesar's old soldiers followed him, and he was the head of all the old political party of Marius. Antony, on the other hand, became more and more disliked in Rome. He lived entirely in the East, where he was altogether under the influence of Cleopatra, and followed eastern habits and customs, which the Romans heard of with disgust. So, gradually, a war came about between Octavian and Antony, which was settled by the battle of Actium in the year 31. This battle was fought at sea, off the west coast of Greece, and was decided by the flight of Cleopatra's ship in the middle of the battle. Antony was so distressed at this that he followed her; and then all his ships, seeing their general run away, turned and fled likewise. Antony was pursued to Egypt, where he attempted to commit suicide on hearing Cleopatra was dead; but she was not dead, and he lived just long enough to see her, but died in time to escape falling into the hands of Octavian. Cleopatra was taken prisoner, but committed suicide by the sting of an asp, or poisonous serpent, which she contrived to have sent to her in a basket of fruit. She was the last queen of Egypt; after her death it was made a Roman province.

THE BEGINNINGS

OF THE EMPIRE

Why the Romans Took One Man as Ruler

So now again the Roman world was under the rule of one man. The murder of Julius Caesar had only led to thirteen years of confusion, and at the end of that time Caesar's adopted son stood in much the same position as his father had stood. Everyone was now tired of these civil wars which had lasted since the times of Marius and Sulla, for more than fifty years. Very few people were alive who had seen these wars begin. Very few had ever known what it was to live under a settled government. So men had lost much their love for the old government of Rome, and were content with any government that would give them quiet and peace, and would bring back law and order. Almost all the chief Roman nobles had been killed in these late wars. There was no family left which could claim to be as great as the Julian family. Octavian was by far the most powerful man in the state and there was no means of getting rid of him or governing without him. After the battle of Actium, when Octavian returned to Rome, the power of the state passed entirely into his hands, and Rome's government slowly changed, in reality though not in name, from being a Republic to being *Monarchy,* or t*he rule of one man.*

How the Empire was Founded

Octavian, however, had learned from the fate of Caesar how dangerous it was to try to change the form of government openly; he had learned that it must be done slowly and quietly. So he never wanted the title of "king," nor did he wish for any extraordinary powers. But he slowly took to himself all the old magistracies, or at least the power of the old magistrates. You remember that when Rome drove out her kings and became a Republic, she did not make any violent change, but at first appointed one yearly magistrate, and then two, who bore the kingly power. Then little by little this power was split up, and pieces of it given to new magistrates. Well, Octavian took to himself all these scattered powers one by one, and so became a king again, though he avoided the name of king. He took the title, *Imperator,* which means *military commander*. It is this title which has been shortened into *Emperor,* and which we now use as the chief title of Octavian and his successors. By this power of Imperator he was head of the army, and the use of this title more than others shows what the new rule was really founded upon. Then he took the authority of Censor, by which he could control the appointments to the Senate. He also was made *princeps,* or *chief man* of the Senate, who always spoke first on every question; from this again comes our title *Prince.* By these powers of censor and princeps he became also head of the Senate. Next he received the tribunician power for life, and as such became head of the people. Then he took the consular power for life, and so was the chief magistrate of Rome. Lastly, he became *chief pontifex, or priest* and so was head of the Roman religion.

Thus he had gathered into his own hands the control over every part of the old government and also held his powers for life. He also had the title conferred upon himself of *Augustus,* or the *Majestic,* just as we say "His Majesty." It is by this name of Augustus that Octavian was always known in his later life.

Rule of Augustus

Augustus lived quite simply at Rome, without any show of grandeur. He kept watch over everything, and always had his own way. He accustomed the Senate and the people to look to him for orders what to do about everything. Sometimes he offered to resign his powers, that they might see that they could not do without him. Once he went away from Rome, and at the next elections there was a riot which only his presence could put down. It was by these means of trying not to give offense to anyone, and of doing everything under the old names, and so not seeming to make any change, that Augustus established the Empire in Rome.

Roman Writers under Augustus

He ruled the Roman world from 30 B.C. to A.D. 14, and the Romans were happy under his rule after all their wars. His reign was the time in which the great Roman writers flourished, and their works are full of mentions of him. It was in his honor that Publius Virgilius Maro wrote his poem of the Aeneid, to tell the great deeds of Aeneas, whose son Ascanius, also called Julus, founded Alba, and from whom the Julian family, to which Julius Caesar had belonged, was said to have sprung. Quintus Horatius Flaccus, and Publius Ovidius Naso, also wrote poems at this time; and Titus Livius wrote his great history of Rome. Augustus was fond of having literary men arond him and used to encourage them to write. Hence it is customary to talk about the *Augustan* age of literature as being that in which there were the best writers, and they were the most highly esteemed.

Effects of the Empire on the Provinces

But the chief thing that Augustus did was the general arrangement of the government. You see that Rome's government up to the time of the Empire had been the government of the people of the city of Rome over all the peoples they had conquered. After the Social War all the Italians had been made Roman citizens, but they could only vote in Rome itself, and of course every man in Italy could not go to Rome and vote every time there was an Assembly. The chief power in Rome was simply that of the rabble of Rome, who came and voted just as they were led by someone popular for the time. The Senate had been always trying to keep this "Roman people" quiet and obedient to itself but had failed to do so. When the Empire was once established this difficulty was settled; both Senate and people had to obey the Emperor. The power of governing the provinces was no longer left to the Roman people, but went either directly or indirectly to the Emperor. Thus, under the Empire, the Italians gradually lost their freedom, and the provincials gradually gained equality with them.

Extent of the Roman Empire

If you look at the map at the beginning of the book, you will see how large was the extent of Rome's dominions under Augustus. After a great defeat in North Germany, he thought that Rome had conquered far enough and that it was only necessary for her to get good strong frontiers. His wars were mostly carried on against the Germans, and he at last succeeded in making the two great rivers, the Rhine and the Danube, the boundaries of the Roman territory. Thus you see Rome's dominions were bounded on the west by the Atlantic Ocean; on the north by the English Channel, the Rhine, the Danube, the Black Sea, and the mountains of Caucasus; on the east by the Armenian mountains, the Tigris, and the Arabian desert; and on the south by the African Desert. Along all this frontier there were only two weak points: one towards the Germans, and the other on the east side towards the Parthians. These two peoples, the Germans and the Parthians, were the enemies whom Rome had chiefly to fear. When Augustus died he left directions to his successors not to increase these dominions; and up to the end of the Roman Empire only two other countries were added. One was Britain, which had already been invaded by Julius Caesar, but which the Emperor Claudius conquered in A.D. 51; the other was Dacia, which was added by the Emperor Trajan in A.D. 106.

New Government of the Provinces

These provinces had been governed, you remember, by those who had been magistrates at Rome and who were purely Roman governors, settling everything in the interests of the Senate. So the provinces had been oppressed and ill treated by many Romans who wanted to make money out of them. Augustus took many of these provinces under his own care and appointed his own governor, who was under his control. Even in the other provinces, which still were under the care of the Senate, Augustus had officers who kept watch over the governors of the Senate. He was always ready also to hear the complaints of the people of the provinces and used to see that justice was done to them. In this way the provinces were delivered by the Emperor from the oppression of the Roman nobles. The provinces before had been looked upon as estates of the Roman people, which they might deal with as they chose, and out of which they made as much money as they could. But now the provinces began to be equal with Italy, and both alike were parts of a great system of government, at the head of which was the Emperor. Instead of being the mistress of all the peoples she had conquered, Rome became only their capital city.

Equality between Rome and the Provinces

This, then, was the result of the change which was brought about when the Roman Republic began to have an Emperor at its head. You see that in this point the emperors went back to the old plan which Rome had followed at first; they did not want to keep the conquered people outside the state and give them no share in it, but they gradually gave the provinces Roman citizenship and so made them all equal to Italy herself. It was because the nobles of the Senate had not followed this plan that they had failed to govern. However, this gift of Roman citizenship did not do much good by itself, as Roman citizens could only vote in Rome itself, and of course men living away from Rome could not go there to vote, however important the matter might be. When the emperors gave Roman citizenship to cities or districts they did not give any real power in the state, for there was no real power except what they had themselves, but they gave the rights of the Roman law and an equal position to that of the Romans who were scattered about as officials through the provinces. So you see the city of Rome first conquered the civilized world and then gradually made all people of the world citizens of Rome, and all these citizens were equal with one another, but all had to obey the Emperor who, however, though he ruled them all, was only a Roman citizen himself.

This was a very curious result of the Empire, and was one that came about slowly; but there was this result at once, that the provinces were better governed. The people were very grateful to Augustus for this. We are told that one day, as he was sailing in his yacht in the Bay of Baiae, a Greek ship which was sailing past saw him. The sailors at once stopped the ship, and, coming to his yacht clad in white robes, they sacrificed to him as to a god, saying, "You have given us happiness, you have secured to us our lives and our goods."

Wars of Augustus

Though Augustus was for the most part busy with arranging the provinces, he also carried on some wars. The most important of these was with the Germans, whom Augustus wished to conquer. At one time the Romans had won all the country between the Rhine and the Elbe, where the English and Saxons were living, but a German chieftain, Arminius, as the Romans called him, attacked the Roman general Varus and destroyed all his troops (A.D. 9). Augustus never recovered from grief at this loss. It is said he used to call out in his sleep, "Varus, Varus, give me back my legions." At all events Germany, north of the Rhine and

Danube, was safe from the Romans, and although wars were made afterwards, they were not wars for conquest, but rather wars to keep down the Germans and prevent them from crossing the Rhine.

Death of Augustus

Augustus died in the year A.D. 14 at the age of seventy-six. He was a very clever man, who had always known how to use everything for his own advantage. He liked to act gently rather than violently; but he shrank from nothing that might help him to get what he wanted. He was not happy in his private life; his daughter vexed him greatly, and at last he had chosen to succeed him his step-son, Tiberius Claudius Nero, who was not of the Julian house by birth, but was the son of Augustus' second wife, Livia, by a former marriage and had been adopted by Augustus as his son.

Accession of Tiberius

Tiberius (14-27) had been extensively employed by Augustus in state affairs and had for the last two years shared Augustus' power. So the Senate, when Augustus was dead, gave him the same honors as Augustus had held, and he became Emperor in the same way. But Tiberius was not as pleasant and kindly as Augustus had been; he was rather stern and sullen, and was fifty-five years old when he came to power, and so was too old to change his ways of life. He did not keep up all the old forms of the Republic as Augustus had done. He did away altogether with the Assemblies of the People for the purpose of making laws; and we must admit that the people who could give up their right so easily did not deserve to have it. 'The Senate also felt itself to be entirely under his power, and some of the feeling of the old Roman nobles again awoke. For the first nine years Tiberius did a great deal of work. He saw that the provinces were rightly governed and that the laws were obeyed. But he felt that he was not liked, and he became jealous of his nephew Germanicus, who was very popular with all classes. So he grew suspicious and tyrannical, and, unhappily, the state of things in Rome allowed him to be as cruel as he pleased.

Evils of the Government of the Emperors

We have seen what was the good side of this new government of Emperors,—the provinces were freed from oppression, and men became more equal. But we must now look at the bad side of it, of which Tiberius and his successors show us only too much. The people who lived in Rome were very different from what they had been in the days when the Roman people ruled for themselves. The old Roman nobles had died out, and in their places had grown up a large body of men who owed their riches to the Emperor, who had not been born in Rome at all, and who cared very little about the old customs. The upper classes in Rome were very rich, very luxurious, and very lazy. The lower classes in Rome were no longer the farmers in Italy, but were a mob of people who had come together from every side to live in Rome, because it was cheap to live there, and there were plenty of amusements. A great part of them had come to Rome as slaves and had managed to be set free. Now this mob cared about nothing except how they could get bread without doing any work, and amusements without paying for them. As long as the emperor took care that they had these, they did not trouble themselves about what he did.

Of course the emperor's power really rested on the army; as long as the army obeyed him he could do what he pleased, and he had a guard, known as the *Praetorian Guard,* of about 6,000 men in Rome itself.

Rise of a Class of Informers

In this state of things the Senate lost its sense of freedom; it had very little to do, and yet its members wanted to have something to make speeches about. So they took to accusing one another of different crimes against the emperor, and they showed their cleverness in finding out new sorts of crimes that might be done against him. Thus, one man was brought to trial because he had melted down a silver image of the emperor to make plate for his own table. At first Tiberius would not allow trials to go on for such charges, but when he had grown suspicious, he used this temper of the Senate for his own purposes. Those whom he was afraid of were gotten rid of in this way. There grew up a class of men who started the trade of *informers,* who got up these charges against anyone whom they thought the emperor would like to see put to death, and who made large fortunes by getting a share of the property of the condemned man. In this way almost all that remained of the Roman nobles were put to death. The rich and distinguished men lived in constant fear that they would be accused. Even Tiberius himself was frightened; he left Rome and went to the little Isle of Capri, where he lived a gloomy and wicked life.

End of the Reign of Tiberius

But though Tiberius had left Rome, he was still regarded as its chief ruler, and this shows you how great a change had already come over Roman ideas. The government of Rome had now become a power belonging to *a person,* and not to the *state.* Tiberius gave his power to others to exercise for him, and Rome was governed by the captain of the Praetorian Guard, Aelius Sejanus, who was very cruel and who hoped to succeed Tiberius. He killed almost all the emperor's relations, till at last Tiberius was afraid of a conspiracy against himself and sent a letter to the Senate, ordering them to make Sejanus prisoner. The letter was a long one and was read aloud in the Senate while Sejanus was there, expecting that it contained the news of some new honor for himself. At the end of the letter was the order to arrest him; Sejanus was instantly seized; all who had been his friends before left him at once; and on the way to prison he saw the people pulling down his statues which had been put up in the streets. He was put to death at once in prison. This will show you how the Romans, when once they had lost their freedom, lost also all their nobleness of character and became mean and slavish and unfeeling. Tiberius died, being gloomy and wretched to the last, at the age of seventy-eight, and everyone at Rome was glad when he died.

Gaius Caligula

But the next emperor, Gaius (37-41), was quite as bad, and shows still more the bad results of letting one man have such great power as the emperors had. He was the grandson, by adoption, of Tiberius, and was the son of Germanicus, whom the Romans had loved so much. He is generally called Caligula, which means a "little boot," and was a nickname given him by his father's soldiers. Caligula became mad when he was emperor. He was always weak-headed, and could only sleep very little, and so his weakness and restlessness, when he had the great power of emperor, led him to give way to the wildest fancies. He had all the ships of Rome put together on the sea across the Bay of Baiae and then covered with planks, on which was laid earth, and trees were planted. Then he rode along this in solemn procession, that he might say he had ridden on horseback on the sea. On things like this he spent so much money that he had to put rich men to death that he might seize their property. So terrible at last was his cruelty that a conspiracy was formed against him, and he was murdered by some of his servants.

Claudius

For a time the Senate tried to rule Rome; but the Praetorian Guard paid no attention to them, and made Claudius emperor, who was brother of Germanicus, and uncle of Caligula. He had always been neglected and looked upon as stupid; in fact, he would have been put to death long before if he had not been despised as useless. The Praetorians found him hiding in the palace of Caligula; one of them saw his feet behind the tapestry with which the wall was hung. He dragged him out and, on seeing who he was, cried out that he should be emperor. All the rest agreed, and the Senate was obliged to give way.

Claudius (41-54) ruled well enough when left to himself, but he did not know how to manage business, and so things were done for him by his wife or his servants, who were all wicked people. In the year 43 Claudius crossed over to Britain, and the conquest of the island by the Romans was begun. Claudius was very good to the Gauls and gave many of them the Roman citizenship; so he was called "the father of the provinces." He had, however, two very wicked wives. The second one, Agrippina, was also

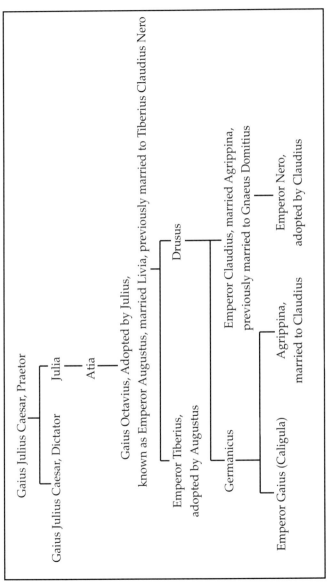

The Descent of the Julian Emperors

his niece. She was a widow and persuaded him to adopt her son, Lucius Domitius Nero. Then she poisoned her husband to guarantee her son's succession to the empire.

Nero

Nero (54-68) is known as a monster of cruelty who put to death everyone whom he chose. He even killed his mother, who had done so much for him. First he tried to drown her by having the ship sunk in which she was sailing, and afterwards, when she was saved from the water, he sent a soldier to kill her. Nero had no care for anything. In the year 64 there was a great fire in Rome, and Nero went up to a hill that he might see it better and fiddled while the city burned. Many suspected that he gave orders to spread the fire farther that it might make a finer sight. Then afterwards the Christians were accused of having made the fire, and many of them were put to death on the charge of general hatred to mankind.

Growth of Christianity

Jesus Christ lived in the time of Augustus and Tiberius, and Christianity had been quietly spreading ever since among the poorer classes all over the Roman Empire. At first the Christians were disliked because they refused to do so many things which everyone else did. All games and amusements were connected with the worship of some of the heathen gods, and so the Christians did not go to them. But there had grown up also, under the Empire, a custom of worshipping the emperor as a god. This may seem strange to you, when you think what sort of men these emperors were; but all the old religions had really died out before Rome's conquering power. They had been national or local religions and had no meaning to peoples who had lost their nationality and become parts of a great empire. So the only thing that men all had in common was obedience to the emperor, and the emperor was the most powerful thing they knew of; so they set up statues to him and worshipped him. The Christians could not do this, and so could not appear at the public festivals, when sacrifices were offered to the emperor. This was the reason why they were looked upon as unsocial and haters of mankind, as well as unloyal to the emperor.

Death of Nero

At last Nero's cruelty could no longer be endured. The provinces grew angry at his doings, and the armies murmured. The Roman people would do nothing for him, and, deserted by everyone, at last he committed suicide at the age of thirty.

Disturbances in the Empire

Nero left no children, and there was no member of the Julian family to succeed him. There now arose the difficult question for the Romans, how the succession to the Empire was to be settled. It had seemed to belong by right to Augustus and to his family by adoption after him, for the Julian family had always been powerful in Rome, and some even thought that it had sprung from the old gods of Rome; but now that the Julian family had come to an end, there was no means of knowing who would be the right man to appoint. The election was held by the Senate, but it could be of no use unless the army agreed.

Galba

The Senate elected first Servius Sulpicius Galba (69), who was general of the army in Spain and a Roman noble. He wished to govern well, but was stern to the Praetorian Guards and offended the man who was most popular with the Romans, Marcus Salvius Otho. Otho expected Galba to adopt him as his son and so to succeed him as emperor, but Galba adopted someone else; so Otho persuaded the Praetorian Guards to rise and kill Galba and proclaim him emperor.

Otho

But the soldiers on the German frontier were not willing to allow the Praetorian Guards to make emperors as they pleased. They proclaimed their own general, Aulus Vitellius, and marched to Italy. Otho and his Praetorians were defeated, and Otho, after a reign of three months, committed suicide (69).

Vitellius

Vitellius was soon found to be of no use as an emperor. He was distinguished only for gluttony and spent all the money he could find in eating and drinking. The soldiers in Syria refused to have him as emperor and proclaimed their own general, Titus Flavius Vespasianus. Vitellius was attacked on all sides, and, after great tumults, in which the city of Rome suffered a great deal, he was put to death, and Vespasian was made emperor.

THE FLAVIAN

EMPERORS

The Flavian Emperors (69-192)

With Vespasian (69-79) begins a new line of Emperors, which lasted for the next hundred years. These are called the Flavian Emperors, because Vespasian was of the Flavian family, and the emperors who succeeded after the death of his sons followed in his footsteps and looked to him as the founder of their power. During these hundred years Rome was governed by good emperors, with only one exception, and the people were prosperous and happy.

Change Made by Vespasian

This was very greatly due to the wisdom of Vespasian, who brought back order to the state and discipline to the army. At first his position was by no means easy, for he had none of the claims to rule which the Julian Caesars had had; he was not sprung from a very distinguished family, nor

120

had he done very great deeds for the Roman people. He was only a good general and a wise and prudent governor of a Roman province, but there were many other men who might claim to be as good as he was. He could not expect any of the old respect for the person of the emperor or any belief in his divine descent. So Vespasian laid all this aside and tried to go back to the old ideas of governing the state, namely, he tried to rule by means of the Senate, to which he paid great honors; he tried to bring back again the idea of the rule of the city of Rome over the world; he always lived at Rome himself and lived as simply as Augustus had done. He did not set himself above the laws, as Caligula and Nero had done, but was careful in everything to obey them.

Thus, you see, he had no claim to rule except that he could rule well; and so he and those who followed him did their best for the prosperity and comfort of the people. But they did no more than this; they did not make the people wiser or stronger or more fit to govern themselves, and so it happened that this prosperous time came to an end, without any fault on the part of the emperors, in confusion and distress.

However, for the time, Vespasian put down the luxury and wickedness which had been growing greater and greater in Rome under the last emperors. By living a simple life himself, he made the senators live better, and by obeying the laws himself he taught others to do the same. We never find after his reign the same wickedness as there had been before.

Titus

Titus, Vespasian's son, put down a rising of the Jews, besieged Jerusalem, and, after a long siege, took it. The

Jews resisted to the last, and the whole city, as well as the Temple, was burned (70). The Jews were scattered through other countries, and the Roman Empire was once more at peace. Titus (79-81) succeeded his father. He was kind and liberal to all men, and was called the "Darling of mankind." At the beginning of his reign there was a terrible eruption of Mount Vesuvius, which destroyed the cities of Herculaneum and Pompeii, and covered them over with ashes. They have now been dug up again, and you can still see there what a Roman city was in those days, as many of the houses still remain almost the same as when they were first buried by the cinders and ashes. Vespasian and his son Titus built splendid buildings, such as the Baths of Titus and the *Colosseum*, which were both open, free of charge, to all the people of Rome. The baths were a sort of club where everyone met and talked, while the Colosseum was a great stadium for games and shows. The emperors had to keep the people in good humor by providing such things for them.

Domitian

Domitian (81-96) was very different from his brother Titus, for he was cruel and gloomy, and took pleasure in bloodshed. During his reign a great general, Gaius Julius Agricola, was carrying on the conquest of Britain. He advanced northwards as far as the Grampian mountains and defeated the Caledonians. After his time the Roman power over Britain was firmly established. Domitian reigned till a conspiracy was formed against him on account of his cruelty, and he was murdered in his palace in the year 96.

Nerva

After the murder of Domitian the Senate proclaimed as emperor an old senator, Marcus Cocceius Nerva (96-98). He had always been very kind and was liked by all. He tried to reign peaceably and to forget all the crimes that had been committed in the reign of Domitian, but the Praetorian Guards rose and demanded the death of the murderers of Domitian, whom they seized and put to death against Nerva's will. But Nerva was determined not to let them do this again; so he adopted as his son and successor to the Empire, Marcus Ulpius Trajanus, who was general of the troops on the Rhine and who would be able to keep the Praetorian Guards in order. Then Nerva died after reigning sixteen months

Trajan

Trajan (98-117) was the first emperor who was not of Roman or even Italian birth. He was a native of Spain, and his family had risen by its merit. The fact that Trajan could now be made emperor with the approval of everyone shows how the differences between Italy and the provinces were going away, and how the government of the emperors was bringing equality among all men.

With Trajan begins a line of emperors who ruled well, and who were great as well as good men. The Romans were very happy under their rule, and the century during which they reigned was looked upon as the happiest time in the history of Rome.

Under these emperors the Empire did not pass on from father to son, but each one adopted as his son and successor the fittest man he knew for so high a place. Trajan set the example of this to those who came after him. He lived in Rome simply and quietly, and was so loved by the people that he was afraid of no one. When he first came to Rome, he came without any soldiers, but simply walked through the streets among the people with his wife. When they entered the palace, his wife Plotina turned and said to the people that she entered her palace contentedly, and would be willing to leave it as contentedly. The Senate, the people, and the soldiers all liked Trajan equally. He pleased the Senate by treating them with respect; he pleased the people by his kindness and his splendid buildings in Rome, where he made a *great forum,* or open square, with galleries all round, and large halls for public business and for libraries and law-courts. In the middle of this stood a tall column with sculptures all over it, showing Trajan's victories over the Dacians.

Trajan's Wars

Trajan was the first warlike emperor. He pleased the soldiers because he was a brave general, and in the year 101 he crossed the Danube and conquered the Dacians, who had long been troublesome neighbors to the Romans. The country between the Danube, the Theiss, the Dneister, and the Carpathian mountains was made into a new province called Dacia.

Trajan was not happy in times of peace, and so he took advantage of a disturbance in Armenia to make an expedition into the East (114). He seems to have had a great plan of conquest there, but after marching as far as the Persian Gulf he came back and died at Selinus in Cilicia in 117. It was very doubtful who was to succeed him, and on his deathbed he is said to have adopted Publius Julius Hadrianus, who had married his niece. Many believed that this adoption had never really been made, but was a fiction of Plotina to avoid any disturbance. However, the soldiers believed it and received Hadrian as emperor.

Hadrian

Hadrian (117-138) at once gave up all Trajan's conquests in the East and went to Rome. It was indeed useless for Rome to try to spread her government in distant lands, where a large army would have to be kept up always at a great cost. Hadrian did not care for war, but spent his time in traveling about the provinces, seeing that they were well governed, and that his troops were well trained. He was the first emperor who did this, and who behaved as ruler of the whole world, and not only of Rome and Italy. He crossed over even into Britain, where he found that the Roman manners and customs had been followed by the people, so that they had become quite like the Romans themselves. To protect the boundaries of the Roman province, he built a wall between the mouth of the Tyne and the Solway, which could easily be guarded by soldiers so as to prevent the northern peoples, who had not been civilized by Rome, from coming down to plunder. In the same way, wherever he went he ordered useful buildings to be built and did all he could for the people. He traveled through almost all the provinces, and we may look upon him as the most useful ruler that Rome ever had. He adopted Titus Aurelius Antoninus, a native of Gaul.

Antoninus Pius

Antoninus (138-161) was called *Pius*, or *the affectionate*, on account of the affection he had shown to his adoptive father, Hadrian. He was a good and kindly ruler who was looked upon everywhere as the "Father of his people." He had been ordered by Hadrian to adopt for his sons Marcus Aurelius, a young man of seventeen, and Lucius Verus, a boy of seven. Antoninus married Marcus to his daughter and gave him at once a share in the duties of emperor, and so Marcus grew up to be the wisest and best of the Roman emperors.

Marcus Aurelius

On the death of Antoninus, Marcus Aurelius became emperor (161-180). He made his brother, Lucius Verus, co-emperor; but Verus was quite unworthy of the position and would have behaved like Nero if Marcus had not kept him back. Luckily he died in 169 and left Marcus free.

Though he was so good, Marcus had a very unhappy reign. He would gladly have spent his days at Rome in study, but he was obliged to leave Rome and spend his days in war. The German peoples now began to cross the Roman frontier. All along the Danube and the Upper Rhine the Romans were attacked by the Germans. The reason of this partly was that the Germans themselves were being attacked at the same time by the Slavonian peoples who lived in Russia, and so they fled from them till they came against the Romans. Marcus Aurelius fought against these Germans and drove them back; but he saw how hard it was for him to do so, and he was unhappy at the thoughts of what would happen afterwards. Another thing which distressed him was that his wife Faustina, the daughter of Antoninus Pius, was a very wicked woman, and behaved badly. Furthermore, his son Commodus did not promise well. So, altogether, Marcus Aurelius saw with sadness that nothing but calamities were likely to happen after his death. He tried to keep them off for a while, but he saw no hope of putting an end to them. He died as he was fighting against the Germans in the year 180 in Vienna.

Change of the Roman Empire

With the death of Marcus Aurelius the line of the good emperors came to an end, and the best days of the Roman Empire were over. No longer was the Empire at peace both at home and abroad, but the barbarians along the frontiers had grown stronger, while Rome's armies had grown weaker. At the same time, also, within Rome's dominions themselves, the people were growing feebler, and the power of the state was falling into the hands of the soldiers. From this time forward the Empire had no longer to think about governing the provinces but about defending them. The old boast that the Roman Empire meant the peace of the world had now passed away. But from this time the Empire stepped forward as the defender of the civilized world against the invasions of uncivilized barbarians. In this way, too, it was the defender of the Christian peoples against the heathen invaders, and this fact led the emperors in time to become Christians themselves.

Commodus

In the reign of Commodus (180-192) the signs of these disasters may be seen only too clearly. Commodus did not care to carry on troublesome wars as his father had done. He went back at once to Rome and there gave himself up to pleasure. The government was carried on by a minister named Perennis, who made himself unpopular with the soldiers; so 1500 of them marched from Britain to Rome to ask that he should be dismissed. He was at once put to death: but you see how powerful the soldiers were growing when they began to interfere in the government itself.

Commodus was cruel and wicked in every way. The thing he cared about most were the sports given to the people. He was very proud of his own skill in shooting, and once when 100 lions were let loose in the amphitheater he killed them all with 100 darts. He used to fight as a gladiator himself, of course taking good care that he was in no danger of being hurt. This was thought very disgraceful by the Romans, and his cruelty was so hateful that at last he was murdered in his palace by his servants.

Pertinax

After his death, an old senator, Pertinax, was made emperor by the Senate, but the Praetorian Guards did not like his sternness. They rose against him and killed him after he had been emperor for three months, and the power now passed into the hands of the soldiers, who made emperors of whomever they liked.

Emperors Elected

by the Soldiers (193-284)

Growth of the Power of the Army

From this time onward for nearly a hundred years the emperors were chosen by the soldiers, and the government of Rome was consequently in great confusion. You remember that it was by the army, after all, that Caesar, and afterwards Augustus, had gained their power. But when they had gained it, they wished to use it with the consent of the people, and so keep it quietly without having to look to the soldiers to help them. Augustus, however, had not been able to do so altogether; he had kept some soldiers, the Praetorian Guards, in Rome; and, as you have seen, these soldiers sometimes settled who should be emperor. Still, on the whole, the emperor was chosen by the Senate and not by the soldiers.

This state of things had lasted while the Empire was at peace, and the emperor lived generally in Rome and was the chief magistrate of the state. But now things were changing, and the emperor had to be the leader of the armies. Marcus Aurelius had been forced to spend his days in the camp, and to try to become a general, though it was greatly against his will. The soldiers were now the most important part of the state, and they would no longer take for their leader anyone whom the Senate sent them.

Confusion on the Death of Pertinax

This was soon found out when the Praetorian Guards rose and murdered Pertinax (193). They then sold the Empire to the highest bidder, who was a rich senator, Didius Julianus This could not be tolerated by the armies along the frontier, which all took up arms. Julianus was killed after reigning three months, and then, after some fighting between the different generals, an African, Septimus Severus, overcame the others and became Emperor (193-211).

Septimus Severus

Septimus Severus was nothing but a soldier and did not care about Rome or the Senate. He governed by force, and was only desirous of keeping the army in his favor. During his reign the soldiers got higher pay and greater privileges, and so became the chief people in the state. Up to this time the Praetorian Guards had always been natives of Italy; but Severus chose them from the best soldiers of all the armies, and made their number 50,000. So now Rome was in the power of these foreign soldiers; and Severus hoped that the emperor, with these troops at hand, would in the future be strong enough to resist the generals of the armies in the provinces. In this way the Empire changed entirely and became a government carried on by the soldiers.

Caracalla

The result of this change was soon seen. The son of Severus, who is known by the nickname of Caracalla (211-217), was a cruel tyrant. He knew that he might do anything, if he only got the soldiers on his side. He murdered his brother Geta, who was emperor with him; and he also went with his Praetorian Guards through the provinces, and so was the first emperor who had been a tyrant anywhere else than in Rome. Thus, at Alexandria, being angry at the jokes which the people made about him, he invited them to come outside the walls and then ordered his guards to kill all who were there. Caracalla used every means to raise money to pay his soldiers, and this was another great evil which this new plan of government brought with it. The soldiers must be paid very highly, and every time the emperor had done anything they did not like he had to give them more money to make them contented. So the people were taxed in every way to pay the soldiers.

Roman Citizenship Given to All the Provinces

One good thing, however, came out of this; Caracalla gave the rights of Roman citizenship to all the provinces, so that all who were governed by Rome called themselves Romans alike. Italy and the provinces were now equal, and there were no differences between one free man and another. This was not done, however, for any good reason, but only that Caracalla might lay upon all the provinces the taxes which were paid by the citizens of Rome. Still this decree of Caracalla was the end of a change that had been slowly going on ever since the time of Gaius Gracchus. It drew the Empire much more together and made it entirely one. Roman ideas had long been spreading among the people of the provinces, but now everyone was in name, as well as in thought, a Roman. People everywhere called themselves Romans, and the name *Roumania* still remains to show how proud were the Dacians, whom Trajan conquered, to mix with the Roman settlers and call themselves by their name.

Alexander Severus

It is not worth your while to know the names of all the emperors from this time. They all met with the same fate; they were set up by the soldiers who had killed the emperor before them, and who needed someone else in his place to give authority to what they had done. Then the soldiers soon found that they liked their new emperor quite as little as they had liked their old one, and so he was killed in his turn. The best of these emperors was Alexander Severus (222-235). He lived simply at Rome and tried his best to govern well. At certain hours in the day his palace was open for anyone to see him who wanted to do so; but a crier stood at the gate and called, "Let no one enter these holy walls unless he feels that his heart is pure and innocent." Alexander tried, however, in vain to lessen the power of the soldiers and to prevent them from committing crimes. They were so strong that they knew that they could do what they pleased without being punished, and were so angry with Alexander for trying to punish them when they did wrong that they conspired against him and killed him. This they did on the banks of the Rhine, where Alexander had gone to lead his troops against the Germans.

Rome's Enemies

It is easy to see that soldiers who made emperors and unmade them as they pleased and who could behave as they chose without fear of punishment were not good soldiers to lead against the enemy. While they were quarreling about which general should be emperor, the foes of Rome were growing stronger and stronger on the frontiers. All along the Rhine and the Danube different tribes of the Germans were attacking the Roman borders. Among them were the Franks, who afterwards gave the name of France to the country which was as yet called Gaul, and the Goths, who were a people closely akin to the English. In the East also a very powerful enemy had arisen, namely, Persians. They had been the great people of the East in old times, when Rome's power did not go farther than her own walls: but they had been conquered by Alexander the Great, and since then had fallen under the power of the Parthians. In the year 226, under a leader called Artaxerxes, they freed themselves from the Parthians and formed again a great Persian kingdom. So you see there had grown up slowly very strong enemies to Rome in the East.

Disasters of Rome

Soon the weakness of Rome and the arrogance of her armies were sadly found out. Rome had now to fight enemies as strong as those whom she had had to do with in her early days, but the soldiers who now fought only to get their pay and enjoy themselves in peace were very different from the Roman citizens who had left their little farms to fight their country's battles. From the year 250 to the year 267 Rome was defeated on every side. In 251 the Emperor

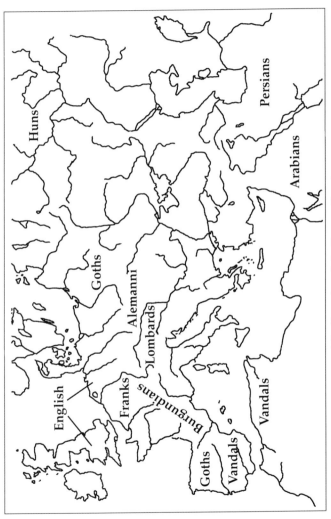

The Enemies of the Roman Empire

Decius was killed in battle against the Goths, and his son Gallus paid them a yearly tribute to get peace. After this the Franks ravaged Gaul and Spain, the Goths plundered Asia Minor and Greece, while the Persians entered Armenia. The Emperor Valerian (253-60) marched to the East but was defeated and taken prisoner by the Persian king. It is said that he was carried about in chains from place to place, and the Persian king used him as a footstool whenever he mounted his horse; when he died his skin was stuffed and kept in a Persian temple. These defeats led to still greater misery in the Empire. During the reign of Gallienus (260-265), the son of Valerian, there arose a great number of pretenders who called themselves emperors. Really the Empire was now broken in pieces; every army called its own general emperor of Rome, and during this confusion there could be no government of the whole.

The Illyrian Emperors

At last, however, the power of Rome arose again. On the death of Gallienus a brave soldier, Claudius, a native of Illyria, succeeded to the throne and drove back the Goths (268-70). After him came Aurelian, another Illyrian (270-75), who left the province of Dacia to the Goths, as he found it useless for the Romans to try to keep it. From this time on the Danube was again the northern boundary of Rome's dominions. But Aurelian again brought the Empire under one ruler. The Roman Empire was still strong enough when it was united and when it had a brave man at its head, but it could only put forth its strength when it was well governed. Every fight for the Empire between generals, every rebellion of the soldiers against the emperor gave the barbarians on the frontiers a chance of crossing the borders and plundering the provinces. Every time they did so the Romans became weaker and poorer and less able to drive them back again. Though Rome might therefore hold out for the present, it was clear she would not be able to do so much longer unless she changed her government for the better.

XII

CHANGES BY DIOCLETIAN

AND CONSTANTINE

D iocletian changed a great deal of the form of the Roman government. His parents are said to have been slaves in Rome, and he himself rose in the army by his abilities. He was made emperor by the soldiers and was determined to keep himself free from the dangers by which the emperors before him had been overthrown. He saw that the two things to do were, first, to defend the frontiers of the Empire from the barbarians; secondly, to defend the emperor from the soldiers, so that they should not be able to put him to death when they did not like him and set up another in his place. He thought that both these objects might be gained by dividing the emperor's power, instead of keeping it all in his own hands. He accordingly chose a brave general, Maximian, with whom he shared the Empire, and who had the title of *Augustus as* well as himself. Afterwards he added two other generals, Galerius and Constantius, who had the name of *Caesars*. The Caesars were not as high in rank as the two Augusti, but they were to succeed to the rank of Augustus when either of the others died.

Power of the Soldiers Reduced

The Roman Empire was thus governed by four men instead of one, and the provinces were divided among the four rulers. Diocletian ruled over Thrace, Egypt, and Asia; Maximian over Italy and Africa; Constantius over Gaul, Spain, and Britain; Galerius over the provinces along the Danube. These four put down all rebellions throughout the Empire and then set their soldiers to work at building walls and fortifying the frontiers. Along the Rhine and Danube, and also along the Persian boundary, camps and castles were built and soldiers were stationed. For a time there was peace and the barbarians were kept back.

This plan, however, only succeeded because the four rulers all worked together. As long as they did this the soldiers had to give way to them; they felt that it was no good to murder only one of them, because the other three would march against them. They would be punished themselves and would not after all be able to choose their own emperor. By this plan the armies were under the emperors' power, and thus, after a long while, Rome had again gotten a government which did not depend entirely on the soldiers.

Seat of Empire No Longer in Rome

One great change which this new state of things made was that Rome was no longer the only capital; other places became as important. In fact Rome was scarcely the capital at all; the Senate still stayed there, but the emperors did not. They lived in places more convenient for them, as they had to be near the frontiers and ready to go to war when they were wanted. Thus Diocletian lived in Nicomedia in Asia Minor, and Maximian in Milan. This change was really a very great one. You have seen that at first the emperors had only claimed to be the chief magistrates of the city of Rome, and commanders of Rome's armies. But under their rule the differences between Rome and the provinces had gradually passed away. Rome had not now the position so far above all other cities which she once had had. The idea of empire was now no longer confined to the city of Rome itself, and the emperors of Rome lived wherever it was most convenient to live.

Magnificence of the Emperors

When the emperors no longer lived at Rome they could make many changes in the old state of things. The first emperors at Rome had lived like the chief citizens, and their houses were simple. This had gradually given way to greater grandeur, and now this grandeur was carried by Diocletian still further. He wore splendid dresses and had a large number of servants; he could seldom be seen by any of his subjects and never did anything without great pomp. People had to behave toward him as if he were a superior being; they had to kneel before him and speak to him in words of great humility. So, too, the names of the different servants of the emperor became titles of rank, which were thought more of than the old names of consul and senator. This grandeur was another method which Diocletian used to separate the emperor from the soldiers. They no longer saw him among them, and they became gradually more obedient to one whom they thought greater than themselves.

Abdication of Diocletian

This, then, was the new form of government which Diocletian brought in and which, as you will see, those who came after him carried out still more. Diocletian is also famous in history because he is one of the very few rulers who have given up their high office of their own accord and have gone back into private life. During twenty-one years he had worked very hard for the state, and, in 305, finding his health was failing, he laid down before the people and the soldiers the purple robe which the emperors always wore, and went away to a palace which he had had built for himself in Dalmatia. There he lived for nine years—but not entirely in contentment, for there arose civil wars among the Caesars and Augusti which lasted till the year 323.

Constantine the Great

In that year Flavius Valerius Constantinus, known as Constantine the Great, once more brought the Roman world under the rule of one emperor. Constantine was the son of Constantius the Caesar, and on his father's death, in 306, he was made Caesar of the troops in Britain. In the wars which followed he was both wise and brave, and managed to spread his power. Gradually he overcame, one by one, all the others who claimed to rule, and so, in 323, he was the sole emperor.

Spread of Christianity

All this while Christianity had continued to spread in the Roman Empire. The number of churches and congregations in every city had been increasing. You have seen that the Christians were not liked by the emperors, and that many of them were put to death by Nero. From time to time the emperors had tried to put a stop to Christianity. They thought that it was teaching the people to disobey the laws and that Christians were not faithful subjects. They could not understand a religion whose followers refused to take part in the religion of the state. They did not object to the Christians having their own worship, but they insisted that all members of the state should take part in the state festivals and sacrifices. This the Christians could not do, and so the emperors from time to time persecuted them. It was not so much the wicked emperors who persecuted as the good ones; for they looked upon the Christians as rebels who ought to be put down. Thus Trajan, Decius (244), and Valerian were all persecutors; but Diocletian was worst of all. From 303 to 313 Christians were put to death in every part of the Empire, but it was for the last time. The constancy with which they endured death rather than agree to what they did not believe showed that they were stronger than the emperors. Through all the Roman world the emperor had brought everything under his own power except Christianity. The Christians alone held out for freedom, and so all those who had any love for freedom began to gather round them. All the old religions had died out; very few really believed in them. The miseries which the Romans had suffered made them feel their need of a religion; the constancy of the Christians when they were persecuted made everyone admire them, and they only grew stronger through the emperors' attempts to get rid of them. So the Emperor Constantine found the Christians so strong that he judged it wise to make the Christian religion the religion of the Empire.

Constantine makes the Empire Christian

Constantine was emperor alone from 323 to 337, and he first made the Roman Empire Christian. This changed it a great deal and made it much stronger; for Christianity bound men together more firmly, and this was very much wanted, since the Empire was beginning to fall to pieces, because there was no great reason why men should want to be governed by the emperors rather than submit to the barbarians.

Constantine Founds a New Rome

Constantine knew this; so he determined to carry out still further the plans of Diocletian and made still greater changes in the Empire. He knew that in Rome itself the old ideas of government would always be very strong; so he founded a new Rome, which was to be his capital city for the future. This city was called, after its founder, *Constantinopolis,* or the *City of Constantine.* It was built on the promontory of Thrace that reaches out into the Black Sea; so, you see, it was on that part of Europe which was nearest to Asia, and also it was built among a Greek-speaking and not a Latin-speaking people. No doubt this was done on purpose, because the people of Asia had always been used to the rule of one man, while the people of Europe had not, and Constantine wanted to make his power more like that which the rulers of Asia had over their subjects.

Also, to do this he had to get rid of the old ideas of Rome, according to which the Emperor was only the chief magistrate of a free people. By building a new Rome, he could take just as much of the customs of the old Rome as he liked and could get rid of what he disliked without making any violent change. It would have been hard to give the Emperor new powers as long as he stayed in Rome; the Senate would still have had a great deal of authority. But in Constantinople a new Senate was formed, which bore the old name but which was filled with men whom Constantine chose, many of whom were Greeks and were used to give in to those who were set over them.

Constantine's Changes in the Empire

Thus the great change which Constantine made was to turn the Roman Empire into an absolute monarchy. He got rid of Rome, its Senate, and its nobility by going to Constantinople. Then he went on to make the army powerless against the Emperor by making the number of troops which obeyed anyone general much smaller than it had been before; also, the troops themselves were divided into two classes, one of which was quartered in towns, and the other defended the frontiers. In this way they were not likely to rebel, because they were so divided that they could not come together in large enough numbers to do any harm.

Besides this, Constantine divided the provinces into a number of small districts, each of which had its magistrates. These small districts again were gathered up into thirteen larger ones. Over these were set four prefects who were answerable to the Emperor. In this way the Emperor became the head of a large body of officials who were put in their places by him and removed by him if he thought fit. Of course all these officials wished the Emperor to go on being Emperor, and so would be likely to keep down rebellions if they could. Also, these officials made up a new body of nobles who took the place of the old nobles. They were nobles not by birth, but because they held offices.

You see, then, how great a change Constantine made. He was very much helped in making it by the fact that he had become a Christian. The new Rome which he founded had a meaning to men as being the first city which had never been anything but Christian. When the great change was made of making the Empire Christian, other changes could easily go with it. People were so glad to have Christianity set up as the religion of Rome that they looked with favor on all that Constantine did.

Evils of the New Plan of Government

No doubt this new plan of government made the Empire stronger. It kept the army in line, and took care of the people. But it cost a great deal of money to keep it going. The Emperor had to live in great grandeur. He had a large court and a very large number of officials, all of whom had to be highly paid. The money for their pay had to be gotten by taxes from the people, and these taxes were paid on the land which every man possessed. But as these taxes were very high, men could not pay them if their lands were ravished by a barbarian invasion. So this plan of government went on very well as long as there was peace, but when there was war on the frontiers the people were brought to great misery. What the barbarian spared the tax-gatherer carried away. So homesteads which had once been ruined were not rebuilt, and thus a strip of desert land was slowly formed inside the Roman frontiers. Of course this did not come about all at once, but things went on gradually in this direction; and you will see what happened in consequence.

Julian

The family of Constantine went on ruling after his death, from 337 to 363. The most important of them was Flavius Claudius Julianus, his nephew, who as a young man drove the Germans out of Gaul. Although he had been brought up as a Christian, he went back again to the worship of the old gods and tried to bring it back among the people. He did not dare to persecute the Christians as other emperors had done, for they were too strong for that; but he turned them out of all offices and made them rebuild the heathen temples which they had thrown down. In spite of this, however, Julian was a good emperor; he made a great expedition against the Persians and defeated them several times, but was killed while retiring from their country. He was the last heathen emperor, but his attempts to bring back the old religion entirely failed; for very few people believed in it, or could do so; really there were only a few men like Julian himself, who were wise men, or *philosophers,* and who saw much worldly wisdom in the old heathen stories and so held to them. Besides these, the country people were slow in changing their old opinions, and heathenism remained in the country after it had died away in the towns; so the word *pagan* means properly one *who lives in a village.* After Julian's time, however, there was never any talk of bringing back the old religion.

The Barbarian Invasions

We now come to the time when the Roman Empire began to be broken up. You have seen how the Germans had for the last 150 years been pressing upon the Romans. Though they were driven back, they became year by year stronger and stronger. From fighting with the Romans, and from being employed as Roman soldiers, they learned a great deal; from breaking into the provinces and plundering the Roman towns they became rich, and also learned Roman habits. The Goths, to whom Dacia had been given up by the Romans, had learned most from Rome, but in 376 they were driven to become Rome's enemies.

Invasion of the Goths

It seems that all this time great changes were going on in the great plain of northern Asia, and in consequence of these changes an Asiatic people called the Huns came into Europe and attacked the Goths. The Goths were defeated by them and were at last driven to cross the Danube and come into the lands of the Roman Empire. The Emperor Valens was weak and could not make up his mind whether to treat the Goths as friends or as enemies. He took them under his protection and then refused to give them food. The Goths therefore rose against him, and he was killed in battle in 378, after which the Goths were for some time masters of the Roman Empire. It is indeed hard to see how the next Emperor, Theodosius (379-95), managed to drive them out. He was a Spaniard who was made emperor because he was the only man who could be of any use. He seems to have been very clever at separating the different tribes of the Goths from one another; and then he fought against them one by one, and at last partly drove them out, and partly made them submit to Rome. They settled in the provinces below the Danube, and so, you see, the Roman Empire had to allow the barbarians to come and take their place within her own borders. This went on still more afterwards, and this is the reason why the Roman Empire was never overthrown, but took the barbarians into itself and so went on changing slowly till it passed away.

SETTLEMENTS OF THE
BARBARIANS IN THE EMPIRE

The Goths settle in Spain

Theodosius was the last emperor who ruled over the whole Empire. After his death (395) it was divided between his two sons, Arcadius and Honorius, in the same way as it had been done in the days of Diocletian. Arcadius ruled in the East, and Honorius in the West. But Honorius was only a boy of eleven and was under the guardianship of a brave general, Stilicho. As long as Stilicho lived he kept back the Goths, but in 408 he was put to death by the order of Honorius, who was afraid that his power was becoming too great. When Stilicho was gone there was no longer any general who could resist the Goths. Under their king Alaric they besieged and took Rome in 410. Alaric died afterwards, and they buried him in the bed of a little stream which they had turned aside for a time and then turned back again, that no one might know where their great king was buried He was succeeded by Athaulf, who had learned a great deal from the Romans. He saw that it was useless to make a Gothic kingdom, as the Goths had not yet learned to obey laws and live quietly; so he thought it better to be friendly with the Romans and to settle down with his Goths among the Roman people. He therefore married the sister of Honorius, and passed on with his army to Spain and the south of Gaul, from which he drove the German tribes which had invaded it. He called himself the officer of the Roman emperor, but he really founded a Gothic kingdom, which was the first regular settlement of the barbarians inside the Roman Empire.

Invasion of the Huns

It was well that the Goths and the Romans were on good terms with each other, for they were soon attacked by their old enemies the Huns. The Huns, under their great king Attila (433-53), burst in upon Europe. They were the worst enemies the Romans ever had. They were of an entirely different race from the peoples of Europe. They destroyed everything wherever they went and looked so strange and horrible that at first the Romans scarcely believed they were men at all, but thought they were more like wild beasts. Attila attacked Gaul and was at last defeated at the battle of Chalons in 451 by an army of Goths and Romans under the command of the Roman General Aetius. Luckily, Attila died two years afterwards, and then the Huns fell to pieces, as their army was only gathered round their leader, and when he died the army did not keep together any longer.

Settlements of the Barbarians

But all this time the provinces of the western division of the Empire were being overrun by German tribes. The

Goths were in Spain and South Gaul; the Burgundians in Central Gaul; the Franks in North Gaul. The English were conquering and settling in Britain, and the Vandals had occupied Africa. Into Italy also the German armies had gone, and although their generals called themselves officers of the Roman Empire, they really did what they chose. At last, in 476, the Emperor Romulus Augustus laid down his title: the Senate of Rome sent to the Eastern Emperor Zeno to say that one emperor was enough, that Italy would have him for its emperor, but that the German general Odoacer would act as his deputy in Italy. So Odoacer, who was a king of the Heruli, ruled over Italy, and after him came kings of other German tribes into Italy, who were all considered the officer of the Eastern Emperor, but who really did what they pleased.

The Roman Empire of the East

All this while the Eastern Empire had gone on more quietly. Attila and his Huns had not plundered so much in the East; they found it better to pass on to Gaul. The Eastern Empire was stronger and kept more together. It differed from the Western Empire, because the people spoke Greek, and had been civilized people long before the Romans were. So they had not become just like the Romans, as the western peoples, who were uncivilized when the Romans conquered them, had become. The Greeks still had their own manners and customs; they were much more busy with trade and commerce than were the peoples of the West. They were very fond of talking and discussing things; so, when they became Christians, they used to dispute about all the doctrines of religion, till the points in dispute were settled by the votes of bishops at a council, and in this way theology grew up. All these things made the Eastern

Empire keep together more than the Western. The Greek-speaking peoples might be invaded, but they did not mix with their invaders; they kept themselves separate and waited till the enemy was gone, and then went on as before.

Effects of the Settlements in the West

In the West, on the other hand, the German conquerors and the Latin-speaking people of the provinces settled down together very contentedly, except only in Britain. The English had never had anything to do with Rome when they came here, so they conquered and drove out the Britons, and would learn nothing from them. But in Spain and Gaul and Italy the people who settled began to talk Latin and to behave like the Romans. And this is why the people of Spain and France and Italy at the present day talk what are called *Romance* languages, that is, languages which began from the Roman but have been changed from the old Latin, because these peoples were careless, and tried to make it easier for themselves as they went on.

Reign of Justinian

So, while the Western Empire was being split up, the Eastern Empire kept together and managed to keep back the Huns and Persians, who were its chief enemies. Under the Emperor Justinianus or Justinian (527-65), there was even an attempt made to win back from the barbarians the provinces which they had taken from the Empire. The great general Belisarius showed a wonderful power of making his soldiers love him and follow him, however rash he might seem to be. He first defeated the Persians; then he crossed over to Africa and defeated the Vandals, and again made Africa a province of the Empire. He then conquered Sicily and drove the Goths out of Italy. Consequently Justinian was real ruler both of Rome and of Constantinople.

But this did not last long, for in 568 another German people, the Lombards, invaded Italy and conquered all the northern part of it. The Persians, too, had become more powerful than ever in the East, and another people like the Huns, called the Avars, settled along the Danube. Still the Empire had great men to help her when she was in trouble. The Emperor Heraclius (610-41) was one of the greatest generals ever known, almost as great as Hannibal. He went with his army into the country of the Persians, and for four years defeated every army they could send against him. The power of the Persians was entirely destroyed; at the same time, too, the Avars had grown weaker, and it would seem that the Empire might have peace.

Conquests of the Arabs

But a more serious enemy was soon to rise against them. Mohammed, an Arabian, taught the people of Arabia a purer religion than they had known before. The scattered tribes gathered themselves together around him and his teaching, and the Arabs went out to conquer as the Huns had done before. There was, however, this great difference: the Huns only followed a great leader, and fell in pieces when he was dead; the Arabs believed what their leader taught them, and so held together while they won a great empire. Syria, Egypt, and Africa were conquered by them, and were never won back by the Roman Empire. One great reason for this was that the Greek-speaking Christians differed very much about questions concerning religion, and when they differed they called one another heretics and quarreled a great deal. Thus it came about that many were willing to submit to the Arabs rather than give up their religious opinions. The Arabs crossed over into Spain and threatened the West but were driven out of Gaul by the leader of the Franks, Charles Martel, in 732.

After these losses, which took place between 633 and 692, the Roman Empire only ruled over Greece, the provinces below the Danube, Asia Minor, and part of Italy. It soon lost almost the whole of what it still held in Italy, because the Emperor Leo III (717-41) quarreled with the Pope, or Bishop of Rome, about the worshipping of images.

Rome Again Sets Up an Emperor

All this time the emperors had done nothing for Italy; the Lombards had become more powerful in the north, and the Popes had made themselves chief magistrates of the city of Rome, as there was no one else. Now, when the Pope and Emperor quarreled, the connection between Italy and the emperors at Constantinople was more and more broken off. The Pope looked to the kings of the Franks, who were the most powerful of the German peoples, and had settled in Gaul, to help him against the Lombards. And at last, in the year 800, Charles the Great, king of the Franks, was crowned Roman Emperor by the Pope in Rome.

The Division of the Empire

At this time, then, there were two Emperors, one at Rome and the other at Constantinople, who both claimed to be the rulers of the whole Roman world, as the early Emperors had been. But really the West obeyed the one, and the East the other; and so men came to speak of an Eastern and a Western Empire. For some time these Empires did not have much to do with one another, and at last they became open enemies.

Fall of the Western Empire

The Western Empire was called at a later time the *Holy Roman Empire,* and its emperor was also the German king. He claimed to have authority over all the people of the West, but his authority grew less and less, as nations formed themselves in Europe. For you have seen that the Roman Empire grew up because Rome brought all the ancient nations under her rule. Then, when the Roman Empire was split up by the settlements of barbarians within it, at first people still all kept together in a sort of way. But the barbarians and the Romans mixed together differently in different places; sometimes there were more Romans, sometimes more barbarians. This made great differences, and so people gathered together into groups according to these differences, and out of these groups sprung up what we now call *nations.* As fast, then, as the *nations* grew up the Empire fell to pieces, and after the Reformation the title Holy Roman Empire meant hardly anything at all.

Fall of the Eastern Empire

The Eastern Empire went on fighting very bravely against the various tribes of Turks in the East, and against the different tribes of barbarians who attacked the provinces along the Danube. It grew smaller and smaller, and became only a Greek kingdom. It was at last destroyed by the Turks, who took Constantinople in 1453, and made it the capital of a Turkish Empire, which still remains.

Influence of the Roman Empire

You see, however, how long the old laws and ideas of Rome went on. Modern Europe was founded on the destruction of the Roman Empire, and the modern nations grew up under its shadow. The power of Rome was so great that it was not destroyed all at once but died away gradually. So you see it is hard to say where Roman history comes to an end. Every nation in Europe owes something to Rome. Some, as we have said, are called Romance peoples, and still speak languages which come from the Latin. Of course, together with Rome's language they also have many ideas about government and other things that come from Rome. The German races, on the other hand, of which the British are one, speak German and not a Latin language. So they do not owe so much to Rome as do the Italians, or the French, or Spaniards, but still they have learned something from Rome, and Roman history must always have a great deal of interest for them, and must teach them to understand all that has happened in Europe a great deal better than they otherwise should.

One great instance of this influence of Rome, even up to our own days, may be seen in the Papacy. When the power of the city of Rome became smaller in governing the State, it began to grow larger in governing the Church. Men had so long been accustomed to look to the city of Rome for laws and government that, when the Emperors no longer lived there, and the Bishop of Rome had become the chief man in the city, men looked to the Bishop of Rome for laws and government in matters of religion. When Rome ceased to be the head of the old Pagan Empire of the world, she became the head of the new Christian Empire of the world: and the notion of the Holy, Roman Empire was that the Pope and the Emperor were closely united, and were together to direct the affairs of Christendom. Long after nations had formed for themselves their own civil government, it was thought that in religious matters all nations must obey the government of the Roman Church. You know that what is called the Reformation is the time in which most of the German peoples, the English among the rest, threw off the rule of the Bishop of Rome. But the Romance peoples still obey the Pope, and though the Roman Empire has passed away in political matters, traces of it still remain in the high position given in religious matters to the Bishop of Rome.

CHRONOLOGICAL

TABLE

B.C.

753   Rome was founded.

509   The Romans drove out their kings.

494   The Plebeians first had Tribunes.

451   The Decemvirs published the Laws at Rome.

396   The Romans took Veii from the Etruscans.

389   The Gauls took Rome.

366   The Laws of Licinius and Sextius made the
      patricians and plebeians equal in Rome.

338   The Romans conquered the Latins.

290   The Romans, having conquered the Samnites,
      became the chief people in Italy.

275   The Romans drove Pyrrhus, King of Epirus, out of Italy.

264-241   First War with Carthage.

219-202   War with Hannibal.

200-160   The Romans conquered the East.

150   The Romans conquered Spain.

140   Destruction of Carthage.

133   Tiberius Gracchus tried to reform the Roman State.

123-121   Gaius Gracchus tried to reform the Roman State.

111-106   War with Jugurtha in Numidia.

102   Gaius Marius drove back the Teutones and Cimbri from Italy.

91-89   The Italians forced Rome to make them Roman citizens.

88-82   Civil War between Sulla and Marius.

74-61   Gnaeus Pompeius overcame Rome's rebels.

58-49   Gaius Julius Caesar conquered the Gauls.

54   Gaius Julius Caesar invaded Britain.

49-48   Civil War between Pompey and Caesar, in which Caesar was conqueror at the Battle of Pharsalia.

48-44   Gaius Julius Caesar put himself at the head of
         the Government of Rome.

   44   Gaius Julius Caesar was murdered.

   43   Marc Antony, Octavian, and Marcus Lepidus
         gained the chief power in the Roman State.

   31   Octavian defeated Antony at Actium and
         became the chief man in Rome.

   30   Octavian, known as Augustus Caesar,
         began governing the Roman Republic as
         Emperor (until 14 A.D.).

A.D.

14-37   Tiberius was Emperor.

37-41   Gaius Caesar (Caligula) was Emperor.

41-54   Tiberius Claudius Caesar was Emperor.

54-68   Nero Claudius Caesar was Emperor.

   69   Disturbances in the Empire after the fall of the
         Julian family.

69-79   Titus Flavius Vespasianus, known as
         Vespasian, was Emperor.

   70   Destruction of Jerusalem.

79-81   Titus Flavius Vespasianus, known as Titus, was
         Emperor.

81-96 Lucius Flavius Domitianus, known as Domitian, was Emperor.

98-117 Ulpius Trajanus, known as Trajan, was Emperor.

117-138 Publius Aelius Hadrianus, known as Hadrian, was Emperor.

138-161 Titus Aelius Antoninus, known as Antoninus Pius, was Emperor.

161-180 Marcus Aurelius Antoninus was the first Emperor who had to spend his time in fighting against barbarian invaders.

192-268 The Emperors were elected by the soldiers, and barbarian tribes invaded the frontiers.

215 The Emperor Caracalla made all men who were governed by Rome citizens of Rome.

268-284 A series of Emperors chosen from Illyria drove back the invaders.

284-305 The Emperor Diocletian made great changes in the Roman Empire.

323-337 Flavius Valerius Constantinus, known as Constantine the Great, made the Empire Christian and built Constantinople as its new capital.

378 The Emperor Valens was killed by the Goths in battle.

379-395   The Emperor Theodosius drove back the Goths.

395   The Empire was divided between two Caesars, one in the East and one in the West.

415   The Goths settled in South Gaul and Spain.

429   The Vandals settled in Africa.

433-453   The Huns, under their King, Attila, invaded Europe.

450-500   The Franks were settling in Gaul and the English in Britain.

476   The Empire was again united under the Emperor at Constantinople, and a German king governed Italy as his deputy.

527-565   The Emperor Justinian made the Empire powerful for a time.

636   The Arabs, united by the teaching of Mohammed, began a career of conquest in Syria, Egypt, and Africa.

800   The Pope, representing the people of Rome, crowned Charles, King of the Franks, as Emperor of Rome.

1453   The Turks captured Constantinople and brought the Eastern Empire to an end.

1806   Francis II abdicated the Holy Roman Empire.